THE CHINA LENS

A Political-Economic Analysis
of Changing China

THE CHINA LENS

A Political-Economic Analysis
of Changing China

SHIWEI JIANG

To order additional copies of this book, contact:
Xlibris Corporation
1-888-795-4274
www.Xlibris.com
Orders@Xlibris.com
127478

CONTENTS

DEDICATION

This book is dedicated to Linda Hyatt Wilson, who started a scholarship to assist a senior researcher in the political-economic studies of China.

PREFACE

This book grew out of a series of my doctoral essays and discussion with Fulbright scholar, Mr. Tasawar Baig and Professor David Earnest at Old Dominion University. Some ideas and thoughts were also inspired by Professor Robert Putnam at the Harvard University John F. Kennedy School of Government and Professor Zbigniew Kazimierz Brzezinski (former US National Security Advisor) when they did lectures and special discussion with me at Old Dominion University in 2009 and 2012, respectively.

In The Third Wave (1991), Samuel Huntington explains various sociopolitical factors caused radical political changes in developing countries. His analysis shows that for Africa, the main obstacle for building democracy is economy, While for East Asia and the Middle East, the major obstacle are culture and religion. Huntington's analysis oversimplified the driving factors of democratization in specific case, such as China, a hybrid of Capitalist economy and communist politics. This paper measures the current democratization of Chinese politics from three perspectives: social capital, rapid economic development and radical social movement. Thus, the grand question is whether these factors can lead to a regime change in China? The author draws a conclusion that the radical political change is possible but not desirable in Chinese politics. In the eyes of rising Chinese middle Class, a Singaporean political transformation or South Korean democratization is more favored than radical democratization.

Following the US Presidential election, China went through a one week meeting of the 18th National Congress starting on November 8, 2012. Without much surprise, Xi replaced Hu, becoming the core of Chinese communist power. The power transition seems to be smooth in Chinese media coverage. However, anecdotes, rumors, unofficial reports and foreign news exposed the political battle behind the stage. President Xi is now facing a stark different situation compared to Hu. Today, China is the world's second largest economy. At the same time, China is experiencing rising mass disturbance every year. As a non-democracy, leaders' past experience, network and personality can greatly influence state policies. With more people getting rich and educated, the mass claim the mismatch between Chinese politics and economy.

Other than changing domestic Chinese politics, China has drawn much attention internationally. China's presence in Africa and the Middle East tightens the nerves of U.S. policy makers. Is China a peaceful or benign riser? Where is China heading toward? What interests are Chinese companies pursuing and what strategies are they using globally? The book investigates these questions in different chapters. Globalization is the current trend. As a propeller, China's participation in global trade greatly shapes world order. In return, global trade also produced effects on China's domestic labor market, particularly on the traditional Chinese women labors. This book is a sound recipe integrating both faces of China domestically and internationally.

ACKNOWLEDGEMENTS

At various stages of research, I got support, either financially or intelligently, from institutions in the U.S. and China. My special thanks go to my educator in China, School of International Affair and School of English at Beijing Normal University (one of the most prestigious universities in China) and my educator in the U.S., Graduate Program of International Studies at Old Dominion University. I would like to also thank several other institutions that played important in facilitating my research. Acknowledgements are due to China National Social Science Fund of Chinese Academy of Social Sciences, China's most reputable social science research institute; China Institutes of Contemporary International Relations and Beijing Academy of Social Sciences. Finally, I extend my gratitude to several superb professors who taught and instructed me in doctoral courses, Dr. Jie Chen, Dean of Dean of the College of Graduate Studies in University of Idaho, Dr. Simon Serfaty, Emeritus professor in Center for Strategic & International Studies and Dr. Regina Karp, Director of Graduate Program in International Studies at Old Dominion University.

CHAPTER 1

Changing Domestic Politics: Democratization and the Multiple Driving Factors

The Changing China: Popular Support and State-Society Relation

What transition has China experienced or is China experiencing? Chen and Shue's books delineate a transitional state-society relation in China. Although the two books focus on different subjects and periods, they are consistent and reinforce each other. The former addresses the popular support in urban China in the late 1990s, whereas the latter addressing the relation between state and rural society in China in the 1970s and 1980s. Chen's book does not discuss the broad relation between state and China's urban society directly. Nevertheless, to some extent, the book scrutinizes the interactive relationship between popular support in urban China and the communist regime. Shue's center-periphery relation of state center and rural society presents us that the state-society relation is an interactive process rather than a monolithic system. Local officials and peasants do not comply with the state's will at any time. For local interests, rural cadres may bargain with the state, even sometimes they "were able to deflect or reduce certain central demands made against them" (Shue, p.45).

What are the Chinese urban residents' attitudes toward their current communist regime? Do they support it? If so, what is the degree of popular political support that the Chinese government now enjoys? These are the major questions probed into in Chen's brilliant work. To maintain its power, the government should either get support from its general public or carry out oppressive policies that tightly control the social order. In non-democratic states and democratic states, what is the difference between governmental maintenance of legitimate power? Apparently, non-democratic states tend to adopt oppressive measures to enhance their regimes. Chen's book can be labeled as typical empirical studies, for it is highly dependent on survey data collected from Beijing in 1995, 1997 and 1999. This is quite different from Shue's book, which primarily relies on historical and cultural analyses.

Chen's book is more systematic compared to Shue's book, and maybe this is because Shue's book is comprised of four articles contributed by different scholars. The systematicness of Chen's book can be readily found in his book. For instance, a systematic research should at least have certain theoretical frameworks to buttress specific cases. Chen clearly lays out his theoretical framework at the beginning. The core theoretical framework of Chen's work is rested on David Easton's classic works regarding political support. According to Chen, Easton subbranches two dimensions of political support. One is diffuse support, which "represents a person's conviction that the existence and functioning of the government conform to his or her moral or ethical principles about what is right in the political sphere, whereas specific support refers to a person's satisfaction with specific policies and performance of the government" (Chen, p.4). In contrast, Shue's book offers various approaches as well as non-uniform theoretical frameworks. It was comprised of different papers by different scholars, such as the approach of "social intertexture of Chinese politics" (Shue, p.4) in the first essay of Shue's book, the center-periphery approach in the second, and the comparative-historical approach in the third.

More interestingly, Chen establishes the correlates of the two types of political support with other sociodemographic factors and attributes such as gender, party membership, occupation, high-politics orientation and low-politics orientation. He carefully examines the distinct concepts of high-politics and low-politics orientation. The former emphasizes democratic values and reform of China's political system, while the latter stresses citizens' satisfaction with living conditions and local affairs. Chen's enlightening findings demonstrate that diffuse support is much stronger compared to specific support among respondents. In other words, the Chinese urban residents support the basic Chinese political institutions and normative values, or Chinese urban residents regard the current communist regime as essentially legitimate. However, the general support for the basic political system is declining. Maybe the mediocre or even poor policy performance gradually erodes the strong diffuse support among residents. Thus, a prominent challenge for the leadership of China Communist Party (CCP) is how to change the downturn trend of diffuse support among the general public. In addition, the low-level specific support tells us that people are not satisfied with policy performance conducted by authorities. Numerous issues concerning citizens' daily life, such as inflation, employment, housing and medical care, are poorly handled by the Chinese authorities. Furthermore, corruption and social inequality also received negative responses from most urban residents.

Some interesting points are put forward by Chen. First, empirical findings from his three surveys indicate that the dominant view that the Chinese regime has lost its legitimacy is not accurate. Second, by far, most Chinese people have considered the regime as legitimate, even though they are not participating in the decision-making process. Chen's implication is based on his findings that the level of diffuse support was higher than that of specific support (Chen, p.52). The Chinese government relies more on diffuse support than on specific support, and this is important for the regime's survival.

Various sociodemographic factors and socioeconomic status are associated with the political support in China. To some extent, it seems that Chinese urban residents construct their own political support quite differently. For those old, male, less educated party members, they embrace a strongly supportive attitude toward the regime. In contrast, those young well-educated urban residents may tend to be critical of the regime and want political reform. As well, nationalism is getting more prevalent among these young urban residents in China as the government propaganda often claims the need for national stability.

Policy implementation and policy performance are poor in China. Social inequalities and corruptions, if not remedied, may lead to increasing anti-regime sentiments that endanger the regime's sustainability in the future. Facing challenges, the CCP, according to Chen, either chooses fundamental political reform, that is, a "genuine democratization" or "provides the public with a more cohesive and convincing set of normative values to justify the existence of the current regime" (p.185). What the

Party has been done is the upgrading of new normative values from Mao to Jiang.

Chen explores the relationship between state and society in urban cities from the perspective of popular political support. Shue explores the state-society relationship in the Chinese countryside. Shue's book expresses dissatisfaction about the prevalent understanding of China's local politics. Former scholars thought that the state center put bureaucratic regulations on the backward countryside during the modernization. Shue observes that some local cadres did not obey the state center's policies and regulations as they pursued and safeguarded their own or regional interests. Local officials in rural China are reluctant to give up traditional habits while basically accepting the state's norms and values. They also consider their own areas' economies more than the state's comprehensive economic plan. According to Shue, local officials in rural China "had acquired such considerable leverage and such skill at evading or distorting central policy that top leaders from whatever faction were greatly handicapped in getting any policy—even one that was generally beneficial—implemented widely as it was intended to be implemented" (p.130). Put simply, local officials' political support toward the central government is contingent on their own local interests.

Different from Chen's empirical studies, Shue's book is marked with cultural and historical studies. For instance, the third essay, "The Reach of the State: A Comparative-Historical approach to the Modernization of Local Government in China" delineates a concise history of the Chinese state, distinct from that of Western Europe. Furthermore, the totalitarian model of the Soviet Union, discussed in the first essay, cannot be applied to explain Chinese state-society relationships because China has the cellular nature of a peasant society throughout its history, which is culturally and historically different from Russian society. Shue argues that the totalitarian approach is static and has little explanatory power for the "numerous shifting, cross-cutting, competitive (even hostile) centers of power" (Shue, p.19). Shue's book also analyzes the change of state-society relation from Mao's rulership to Deng's reform. Unlike scholars' early thoughts, Shue holds that the state's penetration to rural areas was actually quite limited. Rural China was not integrated effectively into the Maoist state. However, later Deng was able to "strip away the honeycomb of entrenched local interests precisely in order to enlarge the reach of the post-Mao state so that the peasantry can be integrated and a modern state established."[1]

Chen and Shue discuss democracy from different perspectives, although democracy or democratization is not the major theme of their books. For instance, Chen discusses the topics of education and diffuse support. He contends that better education seems to have a positive relation with democracy. Chinese intellectuals are more likely to question and challenge the current communist regime. Examples in Chen's book are the May Fourth Movement and the 1989 Democracy Movement (Chen, pp.83, 88). Besides, Chen again involves the discussion of democracy when it comes to the Impacts of Control Variables in chapter six. According to Chen, democratic values and beliefs, which advocate "true competitive elections" and "equal protection," may be incompatible with a single authoritarian party's political and ideological constraints (Chen, p171). Chen expects that democratic supporters are not willing to express their opinions to the authority as voting is viewed by them as "going through a formality (*zou xingshi*)." Furthermore, although Chen does not go deep into the relationship between democratic values and voting behavior in this book, he mentions that the relationship has been confirmed by empirical evidence from his early book co-authored with Zhong Yang. The arguments regarding democracy in Shue's book are comparatively discursive and fewer. However, her book at last puts forward a critical and pointed view, that is:

> In light of 'modernization' in Asia generally, we certainly cannot assume that systemic 'reform', pursued primarily to attain economic efficiency and administrative rationalization, will necessarily bring with them enhanced political influence or democratic freedoms for the masses of rural people. (Shue, p.152)

This argument indicates that democratization and modernization is not necessarily causal to each other. Economic development or modernization highly correlates with democracy sometimes. It is often said that capitalism and democracy go hand in hand. However, modernization may not necessarily lead to democracy in China in the short run. Moreover, this argument makes me wonder what Asian countries, especially China, lack to be democratic, even after they have attained economic efficiency and administrative. Chen and Shue's books inspire us to look into the uniqueness of Chinese politics. Many arguments and concepts presented in their books, to some extents, are culturally and socially bounded within the Chinese society. However, their discussion pertaining to the popular political support in urban China and the state-society relation in rural China does elicit my great interest of delving into the more universal concept—democracy. To explore what makes countries democratic or what factors lead to the political transformation from authoritarian regime to democratic one. Huntington's *Third Wave* and Rueschemyer et al.'s *Capitalist Development and Democracy* offer more detailed answers.

Democratization and the Driving Factors (Cultural, Political and Economic)

Huntington's *The Third Wave*, portrays a holistic picture of the latest democratization happened in the late twentieth century, especially in developing countries or the third world. Many have observed the trend that numerous countries, approximately thirty countries in Europe, Asian and Latin America had experienced political transitions or reforms from the 1970s to the early 1990s. Nevertheless, few addressed this trend systematically as Huntington did. Huntington names this trend "the third wave of democratization". So, what are the first and second waves, according to Huntington? Mainly based on the historiographical perspective, Huntingdon categorizes the three waves by historical events. For instance, the first wave rooted in the American and French revolutions, the second wave started in World War II, and the third wave followed by the collapse of Portuguese dictatorship in 1974. Among the three waves, there are some reverse waves, that is, some countries later changed back to nondemocratic regimes again. However, those reverse waves are temporary. In long run, democratization is still the main trend.

There is certain nuance between Huntingdon and Rueschemeyer's interpretations of democracy. Clarifying the meaning of democracy and democratization is the first step in Huntingdon's book. Spanning from ancient Greek philosophers' seminal thoughs on democracy to the Schumpeterianism in the modern academia, Huntingdon displays his mastery of amalgamating past ideas. Laudably, in addition to reviewing the past literature, he contributes five points to enrich our understanding of democracy. First, the definition of democracy is a minimal definition in terms of election, that is, the meaning of democracy is not only confined to voting and election. Huntingdon puts that "to some people democracy has or should have much more sweeping and idealistic connotations" (p.9). A government is elected democratically by citizens, but it may have poor performance. The poor performance may "make such government undesirable but they do not make them undemocratic" (p. 10). Second, a society may choose political leaders through democratic means, but these political leaders do not necessarily have real power. They may be the puppets or tools of some political groups. Third, Huntingdon touches on the frangibility and stability of a democratic political system. A more democratic political system is not equal to a more stable system. Equally democratic states may differ greatly in their stability. Huntingdon provides the example of New Zealand and Nigeria, that is, Nigeria was once classified as a democratic free state same as New Zealand until the 1984 military coup. Besides, the recent Thailand turmoil also seems to tell that democracy and stability do not have obvious correlation. Fourth, Huntingdon addresses the issue of whether to treat democracy and non-democracy as a dichotomous or continuous variable. The former approach emphasizes the transition from non-democracy to democracy. It also clearly distinguishes democratic states from non-democratic states. The latter stresses the variations in the degree of democracy among countries such as United States, Japan and France. According to Huntingdon, it does, however, have some problems, such as the weighting of indicators (p.11). The fifth point is quite intelligible, that is, nondemocratic states do not have competitive elections and widespread voting participation.

What foster the third wave of democratization? Numerous independent variables may lead to democracy and democratization, such as a high overall level of economic wealth, a strong middles class, high levels of literacy and education, a market economy and so on. Among various variables, no single variable is sufficient to explain the democratization in certain countries. In Huntingdon's words, "democratization in each country is the result of a combination of causes." (p.38)

Huntingdon further puts forward four changes that play a significant role in bringing about democratization wave. First, in authoritarian countries, legitimacy is declining. Military defeat or economic failures may undermine political legitimacy. In the 1970s, many authoritarian regimes had legitimacy problems as democratic values flowed from western countries to the rest of the world. Democratic values are like virus that infected the body politic of authoritarian regimes. In addition to military defeat and economic failures, some sociopolitical issues such as corruption, unemployment, and economic inequality may become the dominant factors that undermine the legitimacy of authoritarian regimes. This is especially true for current China, a country which has increasing military and economic strength as well as worse sociopolitical issues. Chen's book argues that the new Chinese leadership needs to address those sociopolitical issues effectively to boost specific support (p.193). Second, economic development and economic crisis brought down some authoritarian regimes. When a country has continuous rapid economic development, its middle class will consequently be expanded, since education and living standards have improved. A strong middle class is conducive to establish democracy because the highly educated public has favorable attitude and support for democratization. This view is also pointed out in *Capitalist Development and Democracy* which addresses that capitalist development changes the balance of social class power. The middle class is getting power with capitalist development and gradually become a pivotal role in the development of democracy, while working class is not strong enough to push through democracy alone (p.272). On the other hand, economic crisis may accelerate the downfall of authoritarian regimes. The third change that may bring down authoritarian regimes is religious changes. One striking example is the South Korea, which transformed from a society of Buddhism with Confucian overlay to a society with popular Christianity. Fourth, new polices of external factors can stimulate democratization. The European Community and the United States are prominent actors engaging in promoting democratization.

Admittedly, Huntingdon's interpretation of democracy is illuminating. Nevertheless, I do not agree with his views on democracy's implications for international relations. Although, Huntingdon does not use the term "democratic peace theory", he actually elaborates the idea in the book. During the past decades, democracies have not fought with each other. Much world violence came from authoritarian states. Therefore, he thinks that the spread of democracy means the expansion of zone of peace. Moreover, since Russia and China are not democratic states. Huntingdon states that "if, in particular, the Soviet Union and China become democracies like the other major powers, the probability of major interstate violence will be greatly reduced." (p.29)

It is quite doubtful that democracy and war have a causal relation, but I agree that they have certain correlation. Many nondemocratic states fought each in the past because of many complex factors including the political factor of nondemocratic system. However, what is the determining factor that causes wars, national interest or democratic system? It is still unknown. To convince us the reliability of democratic peace theory, Huntingdon should provide more arguments and reasoning. If not, I doubt his argument that if Russian and China are transformed into democracies, the world will become more peaceful. Besides, Huntingdon states that "a permanently divided world, on the other hand, is likely to be a violent world." He thinks that the world today is part-democratic and part-authoritarian. Because of this, the world is unstable. He cited Lincoln's saying that "a house divided against itself cannot stand. This government cannot endure permanently half-slave and half-free." Therefore, he asks a question, that is, how long can an increasingly interdependent world survive part-democratic and part-authoritarian? (p. 29) First, his citation of Lincoln's words is not suitable here. Domestic politics is incomparable to international politics. Second, the world is unstable not merely because the world is part-democratic and part-authoritarian. For instance, an economist may say the world is unstable because it is part-rich and part-poor. A feminist may say the world is unstable because the world is dominant by male power and if there are more women leaders in the world, the world will probably become more peaceful.

Huntingdon analyzes what make states democratic in a comprehensive way. There are cultural, political and economic factors that lead to democracy. It is more like a guide book for students in political science to have a systematic picture of democracy. By great contrast, *Capitalist Development and Democracy* is much more narrowly focused on "the relation between capitalism and democracy or, more precisely, between the transformations of society that came with capitalist economic development and the long-term chance of democratic forms of rule" (p.1). *In Capitalist Development and Democracy,* the authors try to convince us that capitalist development can change a society's class structure—expanding and strengthening the middle class—and therefore advance democracy in the society as the major is now the middle class which is seen as the benchmark and driving force of democracy. Also, in *Governing The Market*, Robert Wade puts "rising affluence and education make for large middle classes, which demand democracy" (Robert, p.343). To some extent, Huntingdon's book neglects the discussion of social class structure and the relation between democracy and middle class. Fortunately, *Capitalist Development and Democracy* makes up this neglect. *Capitalist Development and Democracy* and *Third Wave* share the same background, that is, the return of democracy in 1970 and 1980s gave the research of democratization and democracy an impetus. There are two distinctive traditions of research presented in this book. One is the quantitative cross-national comparisons; the other is comparative historical studies. The authors attempt to fuse the two distinct traditions in this book, according to their statement that the book "builds on the research of both traditions and seeks to reconcile their mythological and substantive contractions." (p.3)

Different from Huntingdon's focus on what makes states democratic, *Capitalist Development and Democracy* emphasize the balance of class power and state-society relations. Moreover, it expresses that increasing organizations and institutions in a civil society are conducive to the establishment of democracy in country because these organizations and institutions have counterweight to state power. China has increasing voluntary informal voluntary organizations and institutions in recent years. However, we do not observe that they greatly promote democracy in China. Why do the increasing voluntary informal voluntary organizations in China have little leverage on the development of democracy? I think the nature, the size and the influence of an organization directly determine whether it is conducive to the development of democracy. The nature of the increasing voluntary informal voluntary organizations in current China is nonpolitical. Most of them are not national. Their influence and size is still limited compared to government-sponsored formal organizations. Therefore, not all voluntary organizations and institutions are conducive to building democracy as *Capitalist Development and Democracy* argues.

Democratization and the Social Driving Factor—Social Capital

Wholly speaking, *The Third Wave* explores the relationship between democracy and culture, politics and economics in a broad way, while *Capitalist Development and Democracy* analyzes the relationship between capitalist development, class structure and democracy in a narrower perspective. Numerous political, economic and cultural variables that affect democracy have been discussed in the above two books; nevertheless, they do not discuss much about social capital that may greatly affects democracy-building.

Social capital is said to first appear in Lyda Judson Hanifan's 1916 paper and 1920 book with a chapter entitled "social capital". According to Robert Putnam,

> "The first known use of the concept (of social capital) was not by some cloistered theoretician, but by a practical reformer of the Progressive Era—L. J. Hanifan, state supervisor of rural schools

in West Virginia. Writing in 1916 to urge the importance of community involvement for successful schools, Hanifan invoked the idea of 'social capital' to explain why."[2]

By far, there is still no fixed definition of social capital. Social capital is distinguished from economic capital and cultural capital by Pierre Bourdieu. He defines social capital as social capital as "the aggregate of the actual or potential resources which are linked to possession of a durable network of more or less institutionalised relationships of mutual acquaintance and recognition."[3] In addition, there are many other scholars who define social capital from differently (e.g. Putnam, Robert. (2000), *Bowling Alone: The Collapse and Revival of American Community*. Portes, A. (1998). Social Capital: Its Origins and Applications in Modern Sociology, *Annual Review of Sociology*, 24, 1-24. Lin, Nan (2001). *Social Capital*, Cambridge University Press). After reading these different definitions of social capital, I feel that the definition of social capital are often referred to collective values of social network, trust, reciprocity, social norms, social cooperation and social resources.

Social capital has tight ties with democracy. Putnam and his followers support that social capital is a key factor for establishing and developing democracy. But not all forms of social capital have positive relations with democracy. Putnam gives us the example of Ku Klux Klan in American history to show that some social capital is destructive for "democracy and social health" (Putnam, p.9).

It seems to me that social capital is favorable for development and modernization in most situations except for some social capital with destructive effect, such as the Ku Klux Klan. Anirudh Krishna's book, *Active Social Capital*, demonstrates three beneficial results of social capital on states. First, social capital helps economic development. Krishna's survey shows that those Indian villages with higher level of social capital perform better than others. Social capital is significant for explaining differences among villages. This is not only true in Indian villages but also in Chinese villages. For instance, Tsai's article presents us four "solidary groups" in rural China, namely, village temples, village-wide lineage groups, village churches, subvillage lineage groups. The former two have higher level of social capital than that of the latter two because the former two are both encompassing and embedding. Therefore, village temples and village-wide lineage groups have a positive impact on local public goods provision, while village churches and subvillage lineage groups do not. [4] Second, social capital is conducive to community peace. More social capital implies more general trust. General trust helps reduce conflicts. Third, high social capital is conducive to participation in democracy. A high stock of social capital assists new village leader to facilitate villagers' participation in democratic governance. (Anirudh, p.169)

Social capital does not foster democracy automatically. For instance, I agree with Chen's finding that social capital is actually abundant in China as there are increasing informal, voluntary organizations in China. [5] However, the abundant social capital in China is not automatically conducive to democracy-building. Up to now, the positive relation between social capital and democracy-building is not that strong in China. Social capital can be classified into formal and informal. I think China has increasing informal social capital, but it still severely lacks formal social capital that is conducive to democracy-building. Besides, Putnam's *Democracies in Flux* inspires me to think that most social capital in China is inward-looking social capital rather than outward-looking social capital. Members of informal voluntary organizations tend to be concentrated on affairs within the organization, and they do not have strong desire to stretch out and concern themselves with the whole society's public goods. Thus, the effects of informal social capital on democracy-building are quite limited in China. However, we expect that economic, cultural and social changes in the future could have more ripple effect on China's civil society, and in return, the transformed civil society may have positive effect on China's political reform.

Conclusion: What are the implications for China?

In the early 1990s, Huntington's analysis shows that for Africa, the main obstacle to democracy is economy-related. For East Asia and Islamic regions, the main obstacle is culture-related. But for China, there are political, economic, and cultural obstacles (Huntingdon, P.134). Twenty years has passed. Hunting's view can still hold war. I think the factors that hinder the building of democracy in China today are still numerous and intertwined. Some political changes have taken place in past decades. For instance, normative values have been upgraded from Mao Zedong Thought, Deng Xiaoping Theory and the important thinking of "The Three Represents" to the current Hu Jintao's "Harmonious Society". There are also some reforms in state organizations and state-owned enterprises. The democracy within the Party and grassroots democracy have been promoted to some extent. However, the Chinese political system has not changed fundamentally. Due to the one-party rulership, Chinese politics Lacks effective supervision. The leadership style is top-down. One of the organizational principles is subordination of the lower Party organizations to the higher.

The rapid development of China's economy gradually expands the middle class, but even today peasants are still the majority. For the peasants, they tend to pursue economic interests more than political rights. For the middle class, they may have come to realize many problems of the current political regime. However, they often compare their living conditions with the past. Thus, many are generally satisfied with the improvement of living standards, and lacks motivation to promote democracy and change the status quo.

Economic factors can promote the development of democracy. In fact, all the selected literature, more or less, touches on the view that economic development has some positive impacts on democracy, and I think most people would agree with this view. However, I think that negative economic impacts on democracy should not be ignored. For instance, the rapid economic development in China today, to some extent, actually further reinforces the authoritarian regime. Additionally, China's new nationalism is not merely the product of government propaganda, but also linked to the economic development. Rapid economic development promotes the rise of new nationalism in China. Authoritarian government can use the achievement of economic development and nationalism to reduce people's advocacy for democracy.

From a cultural perspective, many Chinese with the golden mean of Confucianism (*zhong yong*) are more willing to adapt to the complex bureaucracy and personal connections (*guan xi*) rather than to challenge them. Maybe some hold the view that the CCP's one-party dictatorship is the biggest obstacle impeding the build of democracy in China today, and that if politics has become democratic, and other aspects will correspondingly become more democratic. But, among economic, political, cultural and social barriers, it is difficult to judge which is the biggest to the development of democracy. Even though political democracy is rapidly established, I do not think it is a real democracy because true democracy is a public virtue imbedded in citizens' minds and safeguarded by them, rather than power relations or a form of regime.

The enlightenment that *Democracies in Flux* and *Active Social Capital* provide is that democratic development is not necessarily associated with the abundance of social capital. I think China has abundant social capital; nevertheless, of which little is conducive to democracy. Most institutions and organizations in China are inward-looking social capital rather than outward-looking social capital. Most members are only concerned with the affairs within their institutions and organizations, while few have interest in public good. Meanwhile, China's political system does not allow any informal organization to grow into one with tremendous nation-wide influence. The development of informal social capital is also limited to certain spheres. For instance, no voluntary informal organization can participate in the political sphere. Overall, I think although China has abundant social capital, it is still a static resource rather than an active resource for democracy-building.

Many countries are nowadays labeled as democracies such as India, Indonesia, the Philippines, Mongolia and some other in Latin America because their political system or political form is democratically built up. However, if we look into their societies, we may find that their democratic systems are not well functioned. The people in these societies are not genuine democratic thinkers or practicers. Therefore, I think that the real democracy is not only about voting, election, widespread political participation, political supervision and power relation. It should be a public virtue imbedded in citizens' minds. I hold that the factors impeding the development of democracy in China are multifaceted. The rapid establishment of political democracy in China is unstable and unreliable, while the establishment of real democracy in the whole society is desirable, but it cannot be done overnight.

CHAPTER 2

The Crucial Triangle: The Future of U.S.-Chinese Relations in the Middle East

Introduction

In spring 2006, Chinese President Hu visited Washington and conducted a tough formal talk with his counterpart, George W. Bush. The talk contains many subjects and urgent issues, such as the rebuilding of Iraq, anti-terrorism, global financial system, the U.S. debt and China-U.S. trade, human rights issue and definitely the issue of oil. Hu felt uncomfortable with this visit as Chinese Falun Gong protestor heckled him for several minutes on the White House lawn and besides a white house announcer mixed up China's formal sovereign name (People's Republic of China) with the name preferred by the Nationalist government on Taiwan (Republic of China). By contrast, Hu immediately left for Saudi Arabia after his rash farewell to D.C. and had a greatly cozy atmosphere in Riyadh with the Saudi royal family. Later, it seems that Hu's Arabian sojourn piqued interest in the United States.[6] Americans seem to be unhappy as the Chinese and Saudis signed new oil contracts. To some extent, for the U.S., no matter its politicians or the general public, are getting more and more cautious of the closer relationship between China and the Middle East.

Will China be a challenger to the U.S. in the Middle East? What is the future prospect of the two powers in this region? Will the limited resource lead to China-U.S. conflict in future? These big questions are the mirror of people's concern about the most important bilateral relation in the 21st century, Sino-US relation. It is very challenging to define the Sino-US relation as they are neither friends nor enemies. That is why the smart politicians of the two countries come to coin a tricky word, stakeholder. [7] From Paul Kennedy's *The Rise and Fall of the Great Power* in the late 1980s, to Kissinger's *Diplomacy* in the Middle 1990s and later to John Mearsheimer's *The Tragedy of Great Power Politics*, we observe that the mainstream of international relations theory, particularly the realism is still focusing on the great powers. Despite Keohane, Nye, Wendt, Fukuyama and other scholars in International Organizations or International Political Economy downplay the role of states and criticize the realists' cruelness and pessimism, realism is still embraced by most scholars and students in both academic and diplomatic fields as the mainstream of the IR theory, and this is even true in the media field. Media prefers to report China-US issues in a realist way. It is hardly and impossible to see New York Times, Washington Post or CNN, and Economists report that the Chinese and Americans just hold a great party last week in New York Chinatown. The media is mostly dominated by realism narratives on China-U.S. relation. [8]

Literature review

Mearsheimer is negative toward China's rise and holds that the U.S. should contain China instead of more cooperation and dialogue with it. Mearsheimer is definitely not a dove on the American policy toward China. He advocates thtat the U.S. should strengthen suppressing the rise China through allying other countries. Despite China has not shown any aggressive military ambitions so far, it is inappropriate to make China economically strong via tremendous trades. He worries that China will threaten the U.S. in years to come as it builds up the strong economic base. The rise of China also worries its neighbors, and they are more willing to balance China with the U.S. Put simply, Mearsheimer suggests that the role of U.S. as an offshore balance be strengthened in the 21 century and watch out the rise of China in coming decades.[9] By contrast, Lampton, a specialist of China studies, is positive toward China's rise. He points that "China is not the Soviet Union because it is not placing the same emphasis on acquiring coercive capacity that the Kremlin did during its seventy four year communist history." He holds that we should use China's rise productively, not worry and tame it.[10] In optimists' view, China is an opportunity for the U.S. and China has already been integrated into the American-led international order.

Numerous scholars have addressed issue of a state's rise. Basically, there are two strategic thinking. One is the Sea power theory while the other is the land power theory. Alfred Thayer Mahan's *The Influence of Sea Power upon History* is an excellent piece that illustrates whoever controls the maritime lines, whoever controls the world. The rise of Britain and America prove the credibility of this theory. In the modern times, particularly since the Gulf War, we have witnessed the increasing importance of naval capability. Mahan's sea power theory has tremendous influence in shaping military strategy of Britain, Japan, Germany and the U.S., which finally led to compete in the WWI and WWII. Mearsheimer views sea in an opposite way. He argues that it is the vast water that stops states become global hegemony. He thinks that it is very difficult to occupy other continents because the ocean makes the projection of large number of soldiers impossible.[11] For China, Some scholars hold that China is not merely a land power in tradition. Actually, it was once also a maritime power. They probed into Chinese history and found that China's maritime power was prominent in Ming Dynasty, but later the Qing Dynasty gave up navy development completely and closed the country. Before Columbus and other Westerners started the global adventures, the Chinese had already visited East Coast of Africa, Southeast Asia and India. Besides, at that time, the Chinese ships were 20 times big as Columbus's. [12]

By contrast, the most prominent reprehensive of land power theory is Sir Halford John Mackinder. His heartland theory explicates that whoever controls the pivot area of world land, whoever controls the world. The Middle East seems to be the heartland in the current times. It is interesting to link the U.S. occupation of the Middle East with Mackinder's heartland theory. The importance of the Middle East does not only lie in its rich oil, but also in its strategic location. In a long history, the Chinese kept land-defensive strategy. Building the Great Wall is a perfect example that the Chinese were trying to protect the lands from barbarians in the North. Every year China's Defense White paper claims that China sticks to the land-defensive strategy.[13] Economic development became the top priority Since Deng Xiaopin. A famous Chinese saying once used by Mao and

Deng Xiaopin is "Guang ji liang, Gao zhu qiang, Huan cheng wang", which means "store up grain reserves, build city walls and, in due season, claim the throne."[14] To some extent, this idea has strengthened China's land defensive strategy over the past decades. No Chinese aircraft carrier was made during the past decades.

The Crucial Relation: gradually becoming one of the most important relations in the World

China-U.S.

Sino-U.S. relation is not a new topic. It has been addressed by numerous scholars over the past several decades, such as Kissinger, Brzezinski, David Lampton, and some famous Chinese scholars like Yan Xuetong and Qin Yaqing[15]. Taiwan issue is no longer a sensitive issue between China and the U.S. In Hu's administration, the mainland China actually tacitly recognizes the independence of Taiwan, different from Mao, Deng Xiaopin and Even Jiang Zemin. [16]

What is the current strife? It is the economic conflict which contains trade imbalance, debt, and oil struggle. Oil struggle is a lasting issue between the two countries and will probably become the dominant issue between China and the U.S. in coming 30 years. The Chinese, both government and public, feel very unsecure about their energy security as the U.S. controls the majority of maritime line. The U.S. military is globally present. Americans claim themselves benign power. However, the Chinese do not think so. In many Chinese view, NATO and the U.S. fight for their own interest in the Middle East, not for democracy and justice. Put simply, many Chinese think that the benign power the U.S. is hypocritical. But, when they compare the American domestic political system with the Chinese one, most Chinese would prefer the American democracy. The Chinese have a mixed feeling toward the U.S. On the one hand, the aggressiveness of America and global military intervention can be easily used by the Chinese government and official media to strengthen the Chinese nationalism and the legitimacy of Chinese communist party. On the other hand, the deepening U.S.-China economic activities make more Chinese learn about American political system and society and pose great pressure to Chinese communist party on its authoritarian politics.

U.S.—the Middle East

The U.S.-Middle East relation is much more complex than China-Middle East. It is intertwined with political, economic, military and cultural factors. Radical Islamism or fundamentalist Muslim target at America, not only because America is aggressive, but also because they feel their beliefs are being threatened by the Christian country. On the one hand, America is often criticized for its double standards in the Middle East. America supports Israel unconditionally while shows little sympathy toward Palestine. On the other hand, America is also applauded by many Arabs as it helps sweep dictators. The Middle East seems to be divided into two groups. One allies with the U.S., included in the U.S. led world order, while the other group of states have intense relation with the U.S. and call out Muslim brothers to counterattack the crusade. [17]

Take the 2003 Iraq war for example, he U.S. and some of its allies bypassed the UN and invaded the Iraq. No other states can emulate this. The U.S. did not gain full support from its allies, like France and Germany. To some extent, their relation was hurt by the Iraq War and Bush Doctrine. However, the U.K. is always standing at the side of the U.S. due to the special relation between the two countries. Is Iraq war necessary? This is very debatable. More and more people are getting doubtful of the purpose of launching the Iraq War. Is that for oil? I think invading Iraq is not only for oil. It is mixed with many factors, such as democracy, religion, terrorism and even Bush' personality and his think tank's preference. The U.S. has already spent too much in Iraq. The Iraq is still unstable today but the future is getting brighter as new government and rules are gradually established. It is the time that the U.S. should think about the issue, how to get the war debt paid off and make money from Iraq now? Up to date, American oil companies do not control and monopoly the Iraq oil. Instead, some countries like China actively entered oil market in Iraq and shared the big pizza of Iraq. Americans should keep it up and further show the world that they are there not for oil, but for planting freedom and democracy truly. How to remedy the benign image of America? How to make the world believe that the U.S. is advocating for true justice? It is very difficult but very important for the U.S. after the 2003 Iraq War.

China—the Middle East

China and the Middle East have long tradition of trade. The Silk Road is a perfect example that shows how Persians and ancient Chinese were so eager to exchange silk and spices. Today, China-Middle East relation is simple, but getting more and more complex. The relation is chiefly related to economic and energy cooperation. China does not interfere with politics in this region that much. One reason is that this region is America's "field of influence", the Chinese do not dare challenge the U.S. The other is that the Chinese are culturally more interested in making money rather than religion or politics. Very different from America, Israeli and the Middle Eastern countries, China is currently an atheist society. What the Chinese believe is "face' (mian zi) and money. [18]

In the late 1980s and early 1990s, China was on the early stage of economic development and lacked money and energy. Where to get money and energy? China turned to the Saudis. In order to build up the mutual trust, China sold DF middle-range missiles to Saudi Arab. Immediately, the Saudis got very happy as at that time it became the only state whose missiles range covers the entire region. [19] Since then, China-Saudi relation is developing soundly.

In 2008, the earthquake stroke Sichuan, China. Tens of thousands Chinese died. In the hardship, the Saudis showed their hospitality. The Saudi government and royal family donated $50 million cash to China immediately and later added $ 10 million. By contrast, the U.S. government donated half a million. The Chinese media then started to tease America and praise the friendship between China and Saudi Arab. [20]

According to John Alterman, "It is widely believed in the United States that China supports anti-U.S. governments in the Middle East. The belief is only half true. The People's Republic of China has a history of seeking greater friendship and cooperation with Middle Eastern states that enjoy friendly relations with the U.S. (Saudi Arabia, Jordan, the small Persian Gulf states, Egypt, Israel) as well as states in the region that are or have been locked in conflict with the U.S.".[21] Thus, we should get rid of the distorted idea that China only befriends with the bad guys in the Middle East. Actually, in reality China is trying to build up multidimensional cooperative relations with all governments in the Middle East, which sharply contrasts with America's double standards in this region.

Overall, the Middle East "will need to remain vigilant to the ups and downs in the U.S.-China relationship."[22] States hostile to the U.S. seem eager to encourage a Sino-American rivalry, while others in this region are willing to see a sound and cooperative Sino-U.S. relation. It is predictable that the Middle Eastern states will make a balance between China and the U.S. They will neither always stand with the U.S. nor with China. It is also believed that China's influence in this region will gradually expand from economic sphere to political sphere, because it is impossible to ignore this second largest economy with fast rising military capability.

The Role of Chinese Oil Companies in the Middle East: China's Oil Diplomacy

The strategy

What is China's oil diplomacy? Basically, there are three principles, first, never link oil business with politics, human rights issue, democracy issues and the like. This is the major difference between Chinese national oil companies and Western oil companies. Second, the Chinese government and its central bank financially support the oil-rich states by low-interest loan, debt waiver, FDI and free donations. Last but not the least, China's state-run construction companies actively join local markets in the Middle East. If we take Libya and Iraq for example, we can easily find that several Chinese construction companies are there for building roads, apartment complex, power plant and other infrastructures. With the drastic development of real estate industry in China, Chinese construction companies have gained tremendous profits, skills and experience with cheap Chinese labor workers. They are not only satisfied the domestic market. They are eager to seek new markets overseas. Numerous news come out these days, like Chinese are building giant Casino in the Caribbean, gorgeous mansions in the Southeast Asia, and port in Pakistan and even the Chinese are buying and building lots of real estate properties in New York city recently.

Major Chinese national oil companies in the Middle East

With a large amount of financial aids, the Chinese government encourages Chinese enterprises speed up their internationalization and purchase overseas assets, especially oil assets. Through financial aid, construction and technology aid, it makes Chinese government and oil companies attractive to the Middle East. Chinese oil companies are gradually making China a leader in the oil exploration and production. Among them, three national oil companies are the major players, PetroChina, Sinopec, China and National Offshore Oil Corporation (CNOOC). Their success to entering market in the Middle East is chiefly based on three strategies: first, choose the place where Western oil companies are not willing to enter because of high risk and instability; second, help infrastructure construction, and third, financially backed up by the rich Chinese government.

PetroChina is the China's largest state-owned oil company. Since the mid-1980s, it started to explore the rich reserves of oil field, especially in the Tarim basin in Xinjiang, China. In the 1990s, it began oversea expansion in the efforts to achieve its goal at that time: become a multinational company as soon as possible. At the same time, Sinopec adopted the strategy of "going out".[23] Its business quickly spread to Iraq, Kuwait, Libya and Saudi Arab. CNOOC, China National Offshore Oil Corporation is the third largest oil company in China. It is also the largest natural gas supplier in China. Its oversea business has seen drastic increase in recent years. The three Chinese national oil companies are basically owned by the state. Their executives are thus usually appointed or approved by government official.

Chinese oil companies' strengths of investment in the Middle East

First, it is the political advantage. China's three big oil companies are all state-owned enterprises; thus they usually have more political support and less financial pressure from the state than their competitors, western private oil companies. According to the 2010 American magazine, "Fortune", the PetroChina and Sinopec are listed as the 7th and 10th, respectively.[24] Definitely, they are listed as in the first and second of the China's top 500 enterprises. With strong political support, the three oil companies have gained tremendous brand effect. In the Middle East, PetroChina and Sinopec are prestigious companies, because Arab businessmen and politicians know that the Chinese national oil companies are very stable and robust in investment and will never face financial shortage that some Western private oil companies might have. In most Chinese view, they are also considered to be the most prestigious and profitable companies, where thousands of young Chinese talents are competing fiercely for one position. In terms of market value, their ranking is evening higher. Besides, either in long run or in short term, energy investment continues to occupy the majority of the Chinese government's international investment. Billions of Chinese government's oversea energy investment is practically distributed and operated by the big three Chinese national oil companies.

Second, the overall management advantage of Chinese national oil companies is getting stronger. In 1998, with the restructuring of China's three big oil companies, China's oil and petrochemical industry expanded the original industrial chain to the exploration, development, refining, transportation and other business. Besides, the 1998 reform stimulated Chinese state-owned companies to actively participate in both domestic and international market as the government canceled lots of control and limitation on them and encouraged them to feed themselves. From then, the domestic sales and foreign trade of China's three big companies have been integrated into market-oriented operational system, which increases efficiency and coordination, despite this drew some criticism from thousands of fired workers. With analyzing and learning their competitors' standards and lessons, the three Chinese national oil companies have already become modern super-enterprises. The modernity enhances their international competitiveness as well as provides vast space for their cooperation with foreign oil companies.

For instance, with more than a decade's international operation, PetroChina has already entered the virtuous cycle of the self-accumulation and rolling development stage. In recent years, Sinopec and CNOOC are speeding up the implementation of the "going out" strategy. They are being involved in different scales and different models of cooperation of overseas investment and trade, by participating in project development, construction and management process. They have accumulated many precious experiences out of multinational business operations.[25]

Third, it is the security of Chinese national energy and resource. Along with the national capital accessing to the Middle East, China's oil companies are trying to purchase energy assets there, and to provide financial and infrastructure projects, which attract many Arab leaders. In mining and oil industry, Chinese companies are taking up the upstream assets to ensure the resources and commodities, which can be seen in PetroChina's large investment in oil industry in Sudan and Angola. At the same time, some Chinese enterprises are expanding downstream activities, for instance, CNOOC is turning to retail, petrochemical, metallurgical, and power generation. Oil trade between China and Arab states has enhanced China's national oil security and domestic stability. To some extent, it can be viewed as a kind of collective security.

Fourth, it is the flexible business strategy and comparative advantage of economics. Chinese government and Chinese national oil companies are willing to cooperate with any Arab countries and companies, regardless of its international status, political regime or human right conditions, which created Chinese national oil companies' flexible business strategies in this region. With the support from state, Chinese national oil companies dare to do business in some very unrest region, such as Iraq, Kuwait, Syria, Iran and Libya.

China has comparative advantage in low-cost worker and management, while western oil companies definitely do not have. Tens Thousands of Chinese workers are continuously moved to oil rich countries every year.[26] Although Chinese worker are not as skilled and well-educated as western workers, they are enough economic, capable and suitable to build airport, railway, apartment, hospitals and other infrastructures in the Middle East. The labor cost is considered to be a key advantage that Chinese oil companies have compared to their competitors.

Chinese national oil companies' disadvantage of investment in the Middle East

I think that there is no absolute disadvantage. The disadvantages for Chinese oil companies are comparative. The Middle East has the largest reserve of oil, but most of the Arab states are quite instable. These countries lack skilled labor force. In addition, their communication and infrastructure construction is backward and many living commodities and industrial tools and equipment must be imported from China.

First, Chinese national oil companies do not have mature business strategy. Overall, the three major oil companies lack of unified long-term development plan. There is no clear guiding ideology on how to form a cohesive force in international business. At the same time, the management of their oversea branch is not perfect. Some parent companies do not give oversea branches enough autonomy in operation, so they miss some good opportunities. By contrast, some of the parent companies take laissez-faire attitude toward their foreign subsidiaries, so it is very difficult to implement the overall strategy of the domestic parent company. [27] In addition, most of the state-owned investment lacks of supervision mechanism, often causing unnecessary loss of companies' assets.

Second, Chinese national oil companies face great pressure from domestic energy demand. China's natural resources are moderate; however its population is extremely huge. Therefore, the oil occupied by per person is lower than the world average. With the rise of economy, Chinese are scrambling for oil all over the world, which imposes great pressure on Chinese national oil companies. Besides, as Chinese national oil companies are support by Chinese government and a large amount of their capital comes from Chinese people's taxes.[28] Thus, if they have made any mistakes or failures overseas, they are in the trouble of being fiercely criticized from Chinese public as well as the government. The rising Chinese economy also increases the cost of domestic Chinese labor. The increased cost of exploring new oil reserves may lead to the decline of benefits and motivation to produce. In addition, over the past decade most of the new found oil and gas fields are located in the remote western areas of China. Therefore, the development and exploitation is very difficult there, which needs Chinese national oil company's more investment.

Third, Chinese oil companies are still weak in international competitions and unfamiliar with international practice. In recent years, despite the fact that Chinese oil companies have increased overseas investment in oil exploration and development projects, the oil filed attained by them are either small or falling output, which big Western oil companies are usually not interested in. In addition, since China's oil companies have a lower level of manufacturing technology, lower quality in refined petroleum products, and lower environmental standards. Their efficiency of production is thus lower, which impairs the competiveness of their products in the international market. Furthermore, compared to Western oil companies, Chinese oil companies joined the international oil market late. Thus, they do not have the advantage of first move. They lack talent personnel who have good knowledge of foreign languages and are familiar with international law, international business and management. They lack adequate knowledge and skills to deal with oil countries' political situation, legal characteristics, local culture and customer relationship.

The last but not least is the state-controlled bureaucracy and corruption. According to a report, Chinese national oil companies are facing the following drawbacks. First, they are driven by the promotion of officials, since the company's leaders are not elected but appointed by government. Second, their large investment projects must get the approval from government. Third, the domestic oil price is set by government and they need compensation from the government. Finally, their benefit is very large every year; however Chinese government's taxation on them is very high. Actually, a lot of their benefits have been transferred to governmental revenues. Undoubtedly, in the authoritarian regime, corruption is always a big disadvantage of Chinese national oil companies, which leads to non-transparency of decisions and individual leaders' devour of the state-owned assets.

China's Oil Security: Fears for the U.S. and Navy Transformation

The increasing Chinese oil demand makes China much more nervous about the oil supply security as the U.S. power, particularly the American navy, is globally present and poses potential threat to China's maritime oil transportation. Based on this rationale, the Chinese are speeding up their military strategy transformation, that is, from the land to the sea. According to Jon Alterman and John Garver, Sino-American conflict in the Middle East could cut China off from access to energy, since the U.S. controls the sea lanes on which oil to China travels. [29]

Traditionally, China adopts the strategy of "watching the tigers fight", which comes from an old Chinese saying. This strategy fairly characterizes China's approach to U.S. policy in the Middle East. Partly this is because the Chinese tend to believe that the grandiose ambitions of the United States to control the Middle East and its oil will not succeed in any case.[30] In other words, China is not willing to join the tigers fight in this region, instead China prefers to free riding on the U.S. If the U.S. efforts to stabilizing the Middle East fail, China will probably not step in. Besides, since Deng Xiaopin, China has always kept in mind that economic development is the top priority of national task. The Chinese seems to be good at learn lessons from the ancient wisdom, as I mentioned early "Gao Zhu Qiang, Guang Ji Niang, Huan Cheng Wang.", which means "build tall walls, store grains, and claim the throne later." Therefore, the land-defensive has dominated China's military strategy over the past several decades. Until now, China has never own an aircraft carrier. China's sea projection capability is far behind some major powers.

Here comes the problem, that is, the conflict between the rising oil demand and unmatched navy power. How to solve the problem? Chinese media, general public and decision-makers in recent years seem to embrace Mahan's sea power theory warmly.[31] They call out a transformation of China's military strategy, from land to sea. If we look at several indicators, we will find that China's oil increasing demand is unprecedented. First, China is the second in oil-importing nations, probably become the first in next one or two decades. Oil fuel the rapid economic growth. Once the engine of Chinese economy started, it is difficult to stop or slower it in recent years. Second, as the Chinese are getting richer. The sizeable Middle Class will naturally come into being. Most of them are well educated and to some extent influenced by Western values and live style. They are eager to buy nice cars with larger consumption. This is also rooted in Chinese culture, the culture of face. Owning a new car make them not lose face. It is reported that China ranks the top by motor vehicle production in 2010. Third, China is said to be the second largest manufacturing country in terms of Nominal and the first in terms of PPP.[32] These indicators all suggest that China's economy is fueled and sustained largely by energy, particularly the oil. If there is any emergency of oil security, China will suffer greatly, let alone war with other major powers.

At the same time, the weak navy is always a headache to the Chinese. China has a long history of putting too much focus on the lands. The perfect example is the Great Wall. Ancient emperors made great effort to build the long giant walls to surround Chinese territory, preventing Northern barbarians' attack. However, the Chinese gradually fell behind the Westerners in navy power after the Ming Dynasty (approximately 15th century). In the 1800s, the Westerners opened China's door from the Eastern Chinese Sea. The Great War seems to be left behind since then. Today, the phycology of victim among Chinese, to some extent, provokes the nationalism among general public. The public are pushing the communist government to put more money on navy development. At the same time, the Chinese Communist Party is very willing to see the public support for military development as it can thus gain more legitimacy and control over the authoritarian regime.

Where is the Chinese navy in the ocean? We know that the majority of China's oil supplies pass through the Indian Ocean. But, there is a severe absence of Chinese navy. The public are asking the question, where is our aircraft-carrier? Brazil, India and even Thailand have one or two. The people feel that China deserves one air-craft carrier at least. Again, the Chinese government is good at manipulating the Chinese nationalism in order to strengthen its legitimacy and domestic rule. Despite every year the government publishes the defense white paper, proclaiming that China adopts the land-defensive strategy for peace, it is naïve to think that China will stick to land-defensive strategy forever. The need for protecting business and interest is always associated with the stability and security. As an emerging market and the second largest economy in the world, its military strategy will not be stagnant and unchanging forever.

Based on recent incidents, we have observed that China has an uneasy mood in the sea. First, it is a series of conflicts with neighbors in the South China Sea, like Viet Nam, the Philippines, and Japan. Who owns those small islands is often at the center of disputes. Both sides attempt to prove that they own those islands historically and legally. In the conflicts, American often steps in and tries to make a balance between China and the small states. America is not willing to see that China's navy power dominates this region. Second, China's maritime chokepoints are currently held by Americans, like those essential straits. Despite America states that it will not cut off the oil lane, however the Chinese still lack trust on Americans. In the World War II, Japan failed largely due to the energy cut by American. To prevent the potential crisis on the sea lane, the Chinese plan to bypass the Malacca Strait by creating Pakistan or Burma "energy corridor".[33] To build a canal and port in South Asia or Southeast Asia, China can gain access to the Indian Ocean. Oil then can be transported by land instead of the Malacca Strait in Singapore, where Americans control there. A Chinese scholar puts straightforwardly "whoever controls the Strait of Malacca effectively grips China's energy security at any time." [34]

Based on all, the Chinese attempt to adopt new military development strategy in the 21st century, that is, "Toward Ocean Strategy". In practice, China has already sent navy ships to Africa to fight pirates. Whether it is a justification or not? This is not important. The action shows that China has already improved in its navy strengths. China is trying to transform from a continental to a continental-maritime power in the new era. In the past two years, China did two big things. The first is publicly exposing the Jet 20 When the American Secretary of Defense, Gates was visiting Beijing. The Jet 20 is a stealth jet, which is often compared with American's F22 by military fans. It belongs to the fourth generation of fight jets. Beijing exposed this weapon on purpose, because it will give the Chinese some power when bargaining with the U.S. This year China finally displayed its first aircraft carrier. Again, it is another strong signal to the U.S. and China's neighbors. Mahan's theory seems to be being carried out in China today. Americans and Chinese neighbors are getting more and more cautious of China's next move. For the U.S., Iraq and Afghanistan are almost done, now it has more energy and time to get involved in the pacific region. For China's neighbors, they cannot balance with China solely. Thus, they turn to the U.S. for help. We can see in recent years Viet Nam has greatly improved its relation with the U.S. The Japanese-American alliance is also strengthened. For China, it does not intend to challenge and confront the U.S. on sea directly. However, it feels furious when America interferes in the South China Sea issue. Therefore, we can expect that in coming years, increasing smaller conflicts on sea will emerge between China, its neighbors and the U.S.

Conclusion

Energy cannot last forever. So far, no other energy can match with oil. Oil is cheaper and more efficient. Although electric cars have been developed and encouraged, it takes a long time to see that electric vehicles replace current cars completely. It is very dangerous and pessimistic, if oil runs out before a new kind of effective, massive and affordable energy is popularly used. Therefore, for the scarce energy, oil, big states will struggle to gain and protect in the coming decades.

The Chinese will make effort to build strategic partnership relations with the Middle East. In the process, Iran will be a tricky issue. China needs Iran's oil. Iran needs China's political, economic and military support. At the same time, the Chinese are not willing to hurt Israelis and Americans badly because of Iran. Thus, China will keep certain distance with Iran. Fortunately, for China, Russia is always in the front of conflicts with the Western countries. Since Russia is eager to veto UN resolutions, China just abstains and does not hurt America. I hold that China and the Middle East will get closer, but their relations will not surpass the alliance relation between the U.S. and some Arab states. America is getting more and more cautious of China-Middle Eastern relation. Redressing Bush Doctrine and remedying the relation with the Middle East and alliance is the urgent task for America, no matter through hard power or soft power. The Middle Eastern States are very concerned about the Ups and Downs of Sino-U.S. relation. For most states, they do not expect the worsening Sino-U.S. relation. They wish that the U.S. and China will continue to have a sound and stable strategic partnership, thus they can benefit from it. However, for few states, like Iran, Syria and Iraq, Libya before, they hope China and the U.S. have conflicts so they can gain more support from China. In this way, the Middle East is always a battlefield of games.

The increased oil demand cause Chinese more fear as Americans control the maritime lane and chokepoints. The Chinese are trying to transform military strategy, from land to sea, in case the U.S. cuts off oil supply in future. There is much room for the improvement in the two countries' mutual trust. The increasing Chinese navy power and confidence together with radical nationalists may probably lead to more conflicts on the sea with other countries. China has opened door over thirty years. However, still a large population is poorly educated and informed. They are the force of nationalism. To divert domestic anger and criticism, the Communist Party can make use of those people.

Even though more conflicts emerge, I believe that they will not lead to major war. Nuclear deterrence intertwined economic ties and various exchanges between the two people are the three major stabilizers of Sino-U.S. relation. Compared to those trivial incoming conflicts on sea, the three stabilizers are more decisive and influential on Sino-U.S. relation. I think that new small conflicts are more likely to bring about more cooperation, new institutions, and resolutions between the U.S. and China. Recently, Gen. Chen Bingde, Chief of the General Staff of the People's Liberation Army, led a group of eight Chinese generals on a weeklong getting-to-know-you visit to the United States.[35] It is the first time that a high-level Chinese general is permitted to visit the naval base of Norfolk. This new visit or dialogue is an advance in China-U.S. military relation. I expect that more and more forms of military exchange will happen in the years to come. Finally, the new cooperation, institutions, resolutions, dialogues and forums concerning maritime conflicts between China and the U.S. will gradually shape some parts of the current world order. The world order is always evolving, despite often very slow. It is shaped by major powers and in the meantime it also reflects the interest of great powers.

CHAPTER 3

Probe into the Interrelation between American Interest Group and the Sino-US Economic and Trade Relations

Introduction

In today's international community, Sino-US relation is one of the most important relationship affecting the world, and Sino-US economic and trade relation is a top priority in China-US relations. With the development of economic globalization and China's rapid economic growth, Sino-US economic and trade ties between the two countries have been increasingly strengthened.

With regard to Sino-US economic and trade relations, there are factors of great influence, of which interest group needs to be reckoned. The American political system makes interest group has sufficient space for political activities, such as Political Action Committee, Chamber of Commerce, and National Cable Television Association. Through lobbying, influencing election and multinational companies, legal proceedings and other means, interest groups actively participate in decision-making process with the U.S. government. In U.S. trade policy-making process, interest group also actively plays its political influence to achieve purpose, and to meet its group interests. Based on the importance of Sino-US economic and trade relations, my research chiefly attempts to look at by what means American interest group affect American trade policy toward China. Major questions in this paper are: what is interest group? What is the difference of lobbying among different countries? How to categorize it in terms of Sino-US relation? What is American interest group's effect on Sino-US economic relation? What strategies adopted by two major interest groups, pro-China and anti-China interest groups? What are the implications?

Literature review

What is interest group? There is no fixed answer in academic sphere. American scholar David Truman defines interest groups as "any group that, on the basis of one or more shared attitudes, makes certain claims upon other groups in the society. If and when it makes its claims through or upon any of the institutions of government, it becomes a political interest group."[36] According to Gary Wasserman (1994), interest group is some people organize themselves in pursuit of common interests and exert pressure on the political process.[37] As we can see from the above definitions, to be an interest group, there are three elements at least: first, an organized group; second, group members share common interests or goals; finally, for some common goals, they pose requests to government or put pressure on government in order to make policies in line with their own interests.

In Ronald J. Hrebenar's book (1997), politics in America is often defined in terms of interest group. Ronald's *Interest Group Politics in America* presents some basic concepts and foundations of lobbying.[38] Amy Mckay estimates the ideology of interest group. In his view, political scientists have already developed numerical estimates of political ideology for legislators, parties and candidates. However, they do not pay much attention to the political ideology of interest group. Therefore, he starts to fill in the blank by probing into 72 groups across 10 years.[39] Interest group has tremendous microeconomic or macroeconomic effects. But what are the determinants of interest group? Dennis Coates states that "a nation's stability, socioeconomic development, political system, size, and diversity all appear to contribute to interest group formation."[40]

There are numerous studies in interest group, trade policy and Sino-US relations, respectively. However, few studies combine the above three topics together. Some scholars have already probed into the interaction between interest group and trade policy. Actually, early in the last century, Schattschneider's *Politics, Pressures and the Tariff (1935)* discussed the interest groups' impact on the amendment of the US Tariff Act in 1929-1930. In the 1950s and 1960s, with the emergence of public choice theory and more economic analyses of interest groups' impact on trade policies. More and more studies show that government, the public and individuals have divergent interests. Interest groups can exert political influence and pressure to government policy-makers through many ways. Thus, trade policy is actually viewed as a result of interest group lobbying (Tullock Gordon, 1967). Peter Murrell (1982) tests the effects of interest group behavior on foreign trade patterns. James Sean D. Ehrlich (2008) studies how US trade policies, particularly about tariff, are influenced by political institutions and interest group politics. Walter Lindeen (1970) analyzes interest group's attitudes toward reciprocal trade legislation. Gene M. Grossman and Elhanan Helpman's book (2002) *Interest Groups and Trade Policy* is an empirical study that chiefly addresses the politics of trade in terms of special interest groups. In each country, particularly the US, domestic decision makers receive offers of contributions from domestic special interests. Findlay and Weuisz (1982) think that interest groups can invest appropriate lobbying expenditures to influence government trade policies. Findlay and Weuisz (1982) also assume that some interest groups of imports industry lobby the government to obtain tariff protection; oppositely, on behalf of export industries, other interest groups lobby government to prevent raising tariffs.

According to Marcus Noland, policies are affected by some domestic requirements from various special interest groups (such as import-competing sectors, exporters, human rights activists, etc.) with their own particular agendas. "As a consequence, US policy toward China is probably best regarded as a manifestation of competing interests in which no single goal predominates, and special interest groups may hold sway on particular issues." [41] Robert G. Sutter puts that "the central debates in U.S. China policy during the 1990s have focused on using economic and other leverage to sanction the PRC for human rights abuses or other infractions of U.S.-backed norms."[42] Besides, John W. Dietrich (1999) also did a case study on interest group and foreign policy regarding Clinton and the China MFN (Most Favored Nation Treatment) debates. Other similar research papers are Steven M. Teles's *Public Opinion and Interest Groups in the Making of US-China Policy,* Bibo Liang's *Political Economy of US Trade*

Policy towards China, and Pan Rui's *Politicization Tendency in China-U.S. Economic and Trade Relations as Seen from the Textile Trade Disputes,* which addresses that Sino-US textile trade has always been the focus of trade friction. Sino-US textile trade dispute appears to be economic and trade issues, but in fact, it is the result of multiple factors, such as the US electoral politics, interest groups, trade protectionism, discriminatory trade policies toward China U.S. and etc. Again, there is much literature on interest group and Sino-US economic and trade relation, respectively. However, few scholars scrutinize the two issues in a combined way. This paper attempts to fill in that blank.

Methodology

This research adopts multi-methods from micro and macro perspectives. Waltz' three-layer analysis (individual, society and state) will be applied. From micro perspective, or from individual level, some individuals will be involved in the discussion, such as Clinton and some congress members. From micro-macro perspective, that is, from society level, this paper will involve the pressure of American domestic groups on government, for instance, some American human rights' groups greatly affected Sino-US trade in Clinton administration. American Iron and Steel Institute put forward anti-dumping countermeasure toward China in Bush administration. In Obama's administration, National Association of Manufacturers and American Federation of Labor and Congress of Industrial Organizations (AFL-CIO) exert strong political pressure on president Obama and the Congress to revalue the Chinese currency, RMB. From macro perspective, namely, state level, it will deal with the development of China-US economic and trade relation in the past and in the long-run. To be specific, based on the former two perspectives, I will look at how interest groups and some relevant critical individuals influence Sino-US economic and trade relation. As a whole, this research is mainly based on qualitative method and case study.

Concepts of interest group

Interest group has many names, such as "vested interest", "special interest", "pressure group", "advocacy group", and "lobby group", but these are "negatively charged terms, each implying unsavory tactics or a lack of a concern for a broader public interest."[43] A neutral term should be interest group. In academics, there is a widely cited definition, that is, "Interest group refers to any group that, on the basis of one or more shared attitudes, makes certain claims upon other groups in the society for the establishment, maintenance, or enhancement of forms of behavior that are implied by the shared attitudes."[44]

Besides, Interest group should be distinguished with political parties because their purposes are different: a party attempts to occupy government physically while an interest group wants to influence some decisions made by government. According to degree of involvement in political process (from low to high), interest groups can be divided into social and non-political organizations (American Rose Society, Girl Scouts of America), potential groups (e.g. Christian Coalition) and political interest groups (e.g. Political Action Committee). Potential groups here are "an interesting category of people united by a common interest who are not yet organized and usually are not a regular part of political process."[45]

Difference of lobbying in industrial advanced democracies

In advanced industrial democracies, interest groups have different levels of political involvement. America has the highest level of political involvement of interest groups and largest number of interest groups. European countries' interest groups are still growing and are incomparable to those of America. In America, lobbying activity is incorporated into law and politics. "The ability of individuals, groups, and corporations to lobby the government is protected by the right to petition in the First Amendment to the United States Constitution."[46] Besides, regulating the profession of lobbying in the United States first came in 1938 with the Foreign Agents Registration Act (FARA). The primary purpose of FARA was not to restrict lobbying practices, but to open the books on who pays for lobbying campaigns. [47] In France: lobbying is not integrated in its politics. For example: there is an idea in Rousseau's Social Contract, that is, French republicans are suspicious of particular interests, because they are often conflicted with general interests. In France, organized lobbying just emerged significantly after 1980s. Currently, there is no regulation. In UK, professional lobbying industry grows in recent years if we look at the "revolving door—the movement of personnel between roles as legislators and regulators and the industries affected by the legislation and regulation and on within lobbying companies."[48] Lastly, looking at EU, Lobbying activities are based in Brussels. Most are related to global level, like "diplomatic lobbying". Lobbying in Brussels emerged only in the late 1970s.

Categories of American domestic interest groups involving China issues

Concerning China-US relations, I categorized interest group into four: Trade, labor, ideology and others (see **table 1.**)

1. US government encourages interest groups to participate in decision-making process from the legal perspective. Besides, the diversity of modern American foreign policies provides an opportunity for interest groups to participate in and influence the decision-making of American foreign policy. Meanwhile, the Congress organizational structure is conducive to interest groups' influence on decision-making process. Therefore, the interest groups' role in U.S. foreign policy in is growing. Interest groups lobby the President and Congress to achieve its purpose. Congress's decision and wishes are closely linked to interest groups' lobbying activities. Congressmen formed a symbiotic relationship with various interest groups. They are often the voice of interest groups.

2. Concerning China issues, interest groups are the manipulator of the U.S. Congress's attitudes toward China behind the scene. Different groups involve different special interests in China, thus they hold distinct attitudes toward the development of Sino-US relations.

3. In this paper, trade or business interest groups are called pro-China interest groups, because most of them Support the development of Sino-US relations and push President and Congress to grant China the status of permanent normal trade relations (PNTR). They also encourage more investment in China. The second category is labor interest groups. They are generally against free trade with China. They opposed to large investment in China because it takes jobs away from America. Therefore, it is opposed to granting China PNTR. But this category of interest groups is limited to

economic field. They do not opposite China in all-round aspects. The third major category is ideology interest groups, which are often hard-core anti-Chinese activists and stand at the side of Taiwan. They criticize China's political system, human rights issues and sovereignty problems such as Tibet and Taiwan. Their influence on China-American economic relation is very negative. The last category is other interest groups together, such as various environmental organizations, animal protection organizations, intellectual Property Association. Their concerns are usually non-political, so they have less tremendous influence on China-US economic relations than the former three categories. However, this does not imply that they are not important in China-US relations. Actually, their importance is growing as China and the US have more conflicts in pollution responsibility after China replaced the US as the biggest polluter in recent years.

Table 1

	Trade	Labor	Ideology	Others
Common Interest Groups	American Chamber of Commerce in Hong Kong The US-China Business Council Boeing, At&T, IBM, GE and GM National Association of Wheat Growers North American Export Grain Association Toy Industry Association Footwear Distributors and Retailers of America	The American Federation of Labor and Congress of Industrial Organizations International Brotherhood of Teamsters National Textile Association International Ladies' Garment workers' Union Concerned Women for America	Formosan Association for Public Affairs United Conservatives of America Freedom House National Endowment for Democracy The Southern Baptist Convention Human Right Watch Asia watch	various environmental organizations Animal protection organizations Intellectual Property Association

	Support the development of Sino-US relations Support for granting China PNTR Encourage more investment in China	Against free trade with China Opposed to large investment in China Opposed to granting China PNTR	Hard-core anti-Chinese activists Support Taiwan	Restrain China's development
Attitudes				
Influence on China-American economic relation	Positive	Negative in some aspects	Very negative	Negative in some aspects

Strategies used by business interest groups (or "Pro-China interest groups")

In 1993, the democratic President Clinton replaced the republican President Bush, starting to hold the White House. He changed the status of most-favored-nation (MFN) treatment toward China without additional any conditions ("MFN refers to the normal, nondiscriminatory tariff treatment that the United States provides to virtually all its trading partners."[49]) Under the support of anti-china interest groups in the congress, most senators claimed that the most-favored-nation treatment toward China should be associated with additional conditions. Under this background, the Clinton administration announced that China must satisfy various human rights conditions proposed by the U.S.

American business industries realized this new announcement would hurt their benefits from the Sino-US trade. Their China trade interests were facing immediate threat from the anti-Chinese interest group alliance. Therefore, business industries must unite all the forces that can be united inside and outside government or parliament to change the trade policies hooked with human rights issue. The business interest group had made great efforts to stabilize the Sino-Us relations in this case.

Industry and commerce interest groups did several things for "decoupling" trade polices away from human issues. First, they strengthened coordination between each other, and strove to make the President and the congress clearly understand the United States's economic interests in China. For instance, the US Chinese Chamber of Commerce knew that California has the unique position to the presidential election; therefore it mobilized more than 400 member companies in California to jointly write to President, stating that cancelling the most-favored-nation treatment to China will influence California's $1.7 billion exports to China and that California will thus lose 35,000 jobs. There were lots of similar letters at that time.

Second, Speeding search for Allies in congress and administrative departments and building the united front of "decoupling". Commercial enterprises launched massive lobbying activities toward congressmen in their own districts. They also mobilized a large number of senior members of congress to support the unconditional extended most-favored-nation treatment to China. In May 1994, the democratic Congressman Jim McDermott, from Boeing Company, wrote to Clinton, calling for giving unconditional extended most-favored-nation treatment to China. His letter obtained 106 Congressmen's signature.[50]

Third, strengthening their influence on public opinion and making the whole society to understand China's huge business opportunities and its important influence on Americans' own interests. Industry and commerce interest groups, using *Wall Street Journal, Investor's Business Daily, Business Week* and other national publications, criticized the Clinton administration's trade policies toward that were coupled with human rights. Their views were: first, the best way to change China is to keep economic exchanges and trade with it. Second, the status of human rights issues is too high in foreign policy, and this would ignore some existing important issues in bilateral trade relationship. Coupling trade policies with human rights issues may stimulate a new tide of trade protectionism. Third, coupling trade with human rights ignored the interdependent reality of Sino-US economic. Canceling the most-favored-nation treatment to China was bound to cause international economic fluctuation.[51]

Under the influence of much lobbying from industry and commerce interest groups, a group of congress members who were in the middle-of-road turned to join the pro-China group. Among them, there are senior

Democrats such as Oklahoma's Boren, Massachusetts's Kerry, New Bradley, Louisiana's Johnson and Foley, Florida's Gibenson, McDermott, Erkman and other representatives. Democrat representative Lee Hamilton, former Chair man of Committee on Foreign Affairs, even suggested cancelling the Jackson-Vanik amendment. Hamilton publicly criticized that the Jackson-Vanik amendment were formulated in different times according to different administration to achieve different policy purposes and it was not a good policy to promote China's human rights situation. Lee Hamilton said that Congress needs to consider "how to end this corrosive annual exercise" and grant China the same permanent moststatus that other major trading partners enjoy.[52]

The formulation process of American trade policies toward China was changed in 1994, because business interest groups lobbied relentlessly, pro-China group expanded in the Congress, and American government's economic sectors supported more favorable trade policies with China. For instance, headed by the U.S. Department of Treasury and National Economic Council, the Department of Commerce, Office of the U.S. Trade Representative and Department of Agriculture etc., began to dominate the trade policy making in 1994. Finally, the Clinton administration had to give up previous relevant administrative provisions declared in 1993 and decoupled China-US trade from human rights issues in the end of May 1994.

Since 1993, the rise of American business interest groups changed the force structure of American domestic interest groups of China issues. Anti-China interest groups lost its traditional dominance in Congress. The pro-China interest groups improved Sino-US relations and gradually became the stabilizer between the two countries.

Strategies used by labor and ideology interest groups (or "anti-China interest groups")

First, they made use of American general public's bad impression on Chinese government after the Beijing political storm in 1989. They publicly alleged that Chinese government violated human rights and blamed that American business interest groups just wanted money human and did not think about human rights. More specifically, their publicity includes: first, China forced political dissidents to make goods and then exported to American market; second, China used child Labor and female workers to produce and export products in sweat shops, and their labor rights were not guaranteed. Third, China made use of benefits gained from global trade to strengthen its army and police and etc. Anti-China interest groups voiced against the unconditional extended most-favored-nation treatment to China through multi-channels, such as newspapers, TV, internet and other forms of news media. They also actively attended congressional committees' hearings. For example, in May 1993, there was a hearing held in the House of Representatives. AFL-CIO expressed their opposition against the extended most-favored-nation treatment to China. AFL-CIO used the strategy of "either-or choice". It pushed industry and commerce lobbyists to choose "either conscience or profit." AFL-CIO asked, "Aren't democracy, justice and basic human rights more valuable than those profits gained by exploiting one billion Chinese people?"[53]

Second, anti-China interest groups carried out large-scale lobbying activities on members of congress, especially those conservative congressmen from the eastern states of textile industry. They collaborated and proposed cancelling most-favored-nation treatment to China. They put forward separate Sino-US trade bills and demanded mandatory restrict on Chinese exports to the United States. Under the support of anti-China group, in April 1990, Massachusetts Democratic representative Barney Frank proposed a bill that cut half of China's textile and garment exports to America. In 1991, Congressman Holmes and Gilman (Republicans from New York) proposed a bill that stipulates: ban on U.S. citizens investing foreign penal facilities, and American companies and trade union have the right to sue penal importer and may ask for three times of compensation for loss.[54] This bill includes additional terms against Chinese export. Under this bill, American companies must prove that the products they are imported from China are not made by Chinese prisoners. The amount of the punishment to offenders is high enough for all importers.

In addition, anti-china interest groups continuously notified congressmen and the customs administration forced of the so-called "suspicious Chinese products made by prisoners", forcing the customs to conduct compulsory examination on some Chinese products. Frank, Holmes and Gilman's bills clearly show that trade protectionism groups was one of the important anti-Chinese political action planners and manipulator, human rights was the banner frequently used by the trade protectionism groups.

Third, anti-China interest groups communicated each other in information, mutually aided each other and coordinated in lobby actions. For instance, AFL-CIO provided Laogai Research Foundation in

California a large amount of financial aid. Laogai Research Foundation helped AFL-CIO to collect relevant proof of Chinese exporting products made in forced labor camps. Besides, AFL-CIO aided some human rights organization to supervise China's human rights situation. AFL-CIO leaders also held positions in human rights organizations at the same time, and helped planning activities against most-favored-nation treatment to China.[55]

Anti-China interest groups' lobbying strategies had made great success. For example, with their propaganda, many Americans mistakenly thought that Chinese products were related to human rights. China's export of products made by prisoners to America did not only violate the law of the U.S., but also reflected China's persecution on dissidents. Many Americans did not know the problem of Chinese products made by prisoners was actually exaggerated by American trade protectionism organizations and human rights groups. In addition, many Americans did not know the fact that: When anti-China groups were accusing China of the export of products made by prisoners, at the same time, America was also exporting products that were made by prisoners.

Based on all, a table below summarizes the strategies adopted by the two sides: pro-China and anti-China interest groups and their status of development. (See, **table 2.**)

Table 2

Camps	Strategies	Status of development
Anti-China groups	1. Provide broad media coverage of Tian' anmen incident in 1989. They blame trade interest groups. "Merely pursue money instead of human rights and conscience." 2. Carry out large-scale lobbying activities and cooperate with conservative congressmen from Eastern states of textile industry. 3. Pressure US Customs to have mandatory inspection on certain Chinese products. 4. Anti-China interest groups communicate with each other in the information, mutually support each other in funding, and coordinate in lobbying actions. 5. Influence public opinion on China; sometimes even mislead ordinary Americans by reporting negative news and Chinese political dissents. 6. Exaggerate China's threat theory 7. Protect American labors and win sympathy from general public	Lost traditional dominance in Congress and is Waning.

Pro-China groups	1. free trade with China is good for ordinary American consumers. Jointly wrote letter to President and Congress, specifically asked the Government to extend Most favored nation treatment (MFN) status to China unconditionally 2. American's investment in China and deeper economic relation with China is conducive to China's democracy 3. cooperating with China friendly can gain China's support in many world affairs 4. China's fast economic growth provides many opportunities to American business	Is waxing and competing with its opponent.

The PNTR case

Interest groups usually lobby the Congress and President directly or indirectly to get their favorable motions passed by the legislature. This idea is reflected in the spring 2000 case regarding whether to give China the "permanent normal trade relations" (PNTR) or not.

In early 2000, on whether to grant China the PNTR status, there are two camps. The supporting party is the U.S. business community, farmers and agricultural companies, the Clinton administration, most Republicans, and those who advocate free trade. The opposing party is the American labor unions, human rights groups, environmental groups, veterans associations, most Democrats and anti-China activists.

Members of Congress directly faced the bombing of lobbying activities from the two camps. Therefore, the voting result of the House of Representatives this time is not so much a contest between the members of Congress. Instead, it is more like a result of conflict and compromise between the interest groups behind, namely the labor and ideology group (anti-China) and the trade group (pro-China). This also shows that members of Congress often make resolution or vote under tremendous pressure from interests groups. Their votes may not represent their real thoughts. Therefore, we should simply look at a congressman's vote to determine whether he or she is anti-China or pro-China.

Taiwan's lobbying activities and its new challenge: China Lobby from PRC (People's Republic of China)

This is reflected in the U.S. Congress's policy implementation on the Taiwan issue. So far, Taiwan's lobbying activities are very successful. Congressmen are generally friendly to Taiwan, and often take the initiative to safeguard Taiwan's interests. The reason why US Congressmen are often biased in favor of the Taiwan and put forward a series of anti-Chinese motions are rooted in two aspects. On the one hand, it is the historical relations between the U.S. and Taiwan. On the other hand, it is also because Taiwan is carrying out a lot of lobbying activities on the U.S. Congress. In post-Cold War era, the Taiwan authority has carried out many activities of lobbying the U.S. Congress. Approaches are: 1. in accordance with the laws of the United States, in Washington, employ law firms and professional agents to lobby the Congress; 2. use different kinds of means to win over the incumbent congressmen personally; 3. attending hearing. 4. make use of American Taiwanese; 5. Invite congressmen to travel in Taiwan; 6. provide political contributions like money. [56]

After 2001, the PRC lobby emerged as the Sino-US relation strengthened and US has common interests with China in the War on Terrorism. The PRC lobby has also tried to counter the domestic American interest groups who pressure US government on currency issues and trade deficit. In a word, Taiwan lobby is facing this new challenge—the growing PRC lobby.

U.S. Congressmen's attitudes toward Sino-US economic relation

First, Congressmen's attitude is a key factor to determine the entire view of U.S. Congress toward China. Three categories can be divided into: One is those who always put forward anti-China motion. Account for about

10-15% of the total number of members of Congress, these people are like Jesse Helms, Newt Gingrich, and Christopher Cox. The second is those who have friendship with China, accounting for 30% of the total number. They support China and encourage economic cooperation with China. Third, it is those who have no clear preference on the issue of China and they are easily be swayed by the two types of members above.[57] Second, values and ideological differences matter. The two countries have very different political culture. I think this is a major cause of congressmen's prejudice toward China. For instance, two countries have different understanding of human rights. The American political culture is more emphasize on individual freedom while the Chinese political cultural is based on traditional collective harmony. Third, I observe that there is a pendulum style of the US congress's attitudes on China issues. For instance, in early 1980s, namely, the honeymoon of China-US relation, the Congressmen played a positive role in all-round aspects of Sino-US relations: political, military, economic and cultural. From 1989 to now, in economic and trade aspects, some of them hold positive attitudes toward Sino-US trade. In ideology, politics, and sovereignty aspects, most Congressmen hold negative views toward China.

Conclusion

After the Cold War, China and the US have constant friction and conflict, but due to the rapid development of economic and trade relations between the two countries, interdependence is greatly deepened. China and the US got into a new age of full contact.

In the goals of the US foreign policies toward China, human rights, trade and security interests coexist. The three issues do not appear overwhelming superiority over each other. At the same time, the making of America's foreign policy toward China takes a most outstanding change, namely, different interest groups compete with each other for influencing the policy formulation. Traditional anti-China interest groups have lost its dominance in the Congress since 1990s.

To be more specific, first, there is a balance between anti-China groups and pro-China groups. Neither has predominance over the other. Second, there is a pendulum of Congress members on China issues: usually, economic and trade aspect, congressmen hold positive attitudes while in political, cultural and ideological aspects they often hold negative attitudes toward China. Third, Issues concerning China are actually not a battle between congressmen, but a battle between different interest groups behind. Congressmen formed a symbiotic relationship with various interest groups. Fourth, Strategies by the two major interest groups are similar but competing. As China-US economic relation goes deeper; the new China lobby from PRC is growing and eroding the old Taiwan lobby. Finally, take the most-favored-nation treatment for example; two competing alliances regarding China issues have been formed in the US since 1990s. One is the anti-China interests groups that are composed of political conservatives and organizations of human rights (ideology) and Labor. The other alliance is pro-China interest groups which support stable Sino-US relationship and are majorly composed of business individuals or organizations. Industrial and commercial interest groups or business interest groups are the stabilizer of Sino-US economic relation.

In the past, in our researches we often paid much attention to examining the relationship between Congress and the President, but relatively ignoring American domestic interest groups' role on American foreign policy toward China. Post-Cold War Changes require us to strengthen the study of American interests group and Sino-US relations and pay close attention to the waxing and waning of American interest groups' forces. My suggestion to China is that Chinese political and business groups ought to actively contact the US Congressmen while obeying relevant American laws, and thus improve their understanding of China and make them recognize the great benefits of the stability of Sino-US relation. Anti-China interest groups today are overshadowed by Sino-US trade. They also have some problems, such as capital insufficiency, loose organization, and relative disadvantage of competition with those big pro-China companies like Boeing. However, they reflect the basic value orientation of some grass-roots Americans, namely, negative views toward Chinese ideology, politics and trade deficit. Therefore, we still cannot exclude the possibility of the resurgence of anti-China tide in America in future.

CHAPTER 4

China's Scramble for African Oil: A SWOT Analysis of Chinese National Oil Corporations in Africa

Introduction

In many Chinese people's view, Africa has great potential in oil in future. Since 2006, Angola has become the top source of crude oil imports to China, replacing Saudi Arabia. [58]Actually, this is not a big surprise. The Western countries have dominant influence in the Middle East and Chinese government and national oil companies are always worrying about that. Particularly, after the 2003 Iraq war, the Chinese government realized that it should immediately diversify its oil sources in order to reduce the risks brought by America's military intervention and control in the Middle East. In some Chinese narratives, some Middle East countries are viewed as the "puppets" of the world police, America.[59] The negative narratives actually stimulate many Chinese nationalists' strong support for government's decision of reducing the oil dependence on the Middle East and speeding up China's scramble for African oil. With the rise of oil business in Africa, many people will ask what obstacles and opportunities do Chinese oil companies have there.

To answer this major question, in this article, the SWOT analysis of enterprise is adopted. An enterprise's internal and external environment is viewed as an important component of its strategic planning process. This analytical method can provide useful information for matching the enterprise's resource capacity and the competitive environment. From basic principles of resources mercantilist view,[60] China's three big oil companies, PetroChina, Sinopec and China and National Offshore Oil Corporation (CNOOC), formed a new prototype of investment and operation in the global oil market, which has very different characteristics from the Western oil giants. A SWOT analysis helps us probe into and understand these characteristics. This article is chiefly composed of four parts. The first section is the literature review of oil companies entering and investing in foreign markets. The second section is a brief introduction of Major Chinese national oil companies' overall business in Africa. The third section is the main body of this article, the SWOT analysis of three Chinese national oil companies in Africa. The last section is the conclusion.

Literature review

In the past, when it comes to oil and security, lots of scholars focus on the Middle East oil trade and security. There are a sea of literatures and studies on the Middle East and Oil. By contrast, the study on China-Africa oil trade is a recent topic as China speeds up finding new sources of oil after the Iraq War. Numerous studies on China's oil business in Africa are emerging. Most of them focus on Chinese government's oil policies and oil diplomacy in Africa. Two Chinese scholars, Cheng J and Shi H (2009), examined the overall African policy of China after the Cold War. They point out that "Chinese leaders have no intention of engaging in diplomatic and strategic competition with the USA and the European Union in Africa." Another Chinese scholar, Wu (2009) narrowed down the period to 2003-2008 and studied China's oil diplomacy toward Africa, which argues that the U.S. and China indeed compete for African oil, but there is much room for cooperation in future. Besides, Ian Taylor's China's Oil diplomacy in Africa and China's new role in Africa conduct more systemic study on Chinese government's stance on African oil. Other than oil diplomacy in Africa, some scholars also analyze China's oil challenges in Africa, such as Sarah Raine's *The rise of China and India in Africa: challenges, opportunities and critical interventions*, Lucy Corkin's *Uneasy allies: China's evolving relations with Angola*, Fantu Cheru's *China returns to Africa: a rising power and a continent embrace*. In addition, some scholars look at China's competition in Africa oil, particularly the competitions with the U.S. The prominent publications include Z Zhang's "China's Hunt for Oil in Africa in Perspective", Michael Klare and Daniel Volman's "America, China & the Scramble for Africa's Oil", Peter Marton and Tamas Matura's "The 'voracious dragon', the 'scramble' and the 'honey pot': Conceptions of conflict over Africa's natural resources" and Callie Amanda Wang's "Fueling the fire?: Civil war in Africa and the People's Republic of China." Overall, a lot of the current literature focuses too broadly on the state and government level and to some extent has ignore the Chinese oil companies in Africa. What are the differences of oil business in Africa between Chinese oil companies and Western oil companies? What are the strengths and weakness of Chinese oil companies, and what are the obstacle and challenges they are facing there? Little literature narrowly focused on the major Chinese national oil companies themselves and addressed these questions systemically. To answer the above questions, the SWOT analytical approach is suitable to be adopted. This approach is "credited to two Harvard Business School Policy Unit professors George Albert Smith Jr and C Roland Christiensen during the early 1950s."[61] It is also applied by Stanford University's Albert Humphrey in the 1960s and 1970s. Nowadays, it has been widely used and tested in the subject of management and marketing. Clearly, the focus of this article is neither on the Chinese government nor the oil diplomacy and oil security at state level; rather it is narrowly concentrating on the characteristics of three major Chinese national oil companies.

Major Chinese national oil companies in Africa

With a large amount of financial aids, the Chinese government encourages Chinese enterprises speed up their internationalization and purchase overseas assets, especially oil assets. Through generous loans and credit means, it makes African governments loyal to the project contract funded by the Chinese government and oil companies. The below statistics by Houser (2008) shows that Chinese National oil companies have greater investment interest in Africa than other regions.[62]

Chinese oil companies make China become a leader in Africa oil exploration and production. Among them, three national oil companies are the major players, PetroChina, Sinopec, and CNOOC. Their success to entering market in Africa is chiefly based on three strategies: first, choose the place where Western oil companies are not willing to enter because of high risk and instability; second, help infrastructure construction, and third, provide financial aid donations.

1. PetroChina

Petrochina is China's largest state-owned oil company. Since the mid-1980s, it started to explore the rich reserves of oil field, especially in the Tarim basin in Xinjiang, China. In the 1990s, it began oversea expansion in the efforts to achieve its goal at that time: become a multinational company as soon as possible. In 1997, it defeated other international oil companies and won the exploitation rights of Muglad basin in Sudan. This is the first time that PetroChina successfully bid the large-scale overseas oil and gas exploration project. To some extent, Sudan is the starting point that PetroChina started its global competition. [63]

2. Sinopec

Sinopec adopted the strategy of "going out". In 2004, Sinopec signed an evaluation deal with Gabon. During his African visit that year Chinese President Hu Jintao signed a series of bilateral trade accords with his Gabonese counterpart Omar Bongo, including a "memorandum of agreement aimed at showing the parties' desire to develop exploration, exploitation, refining and export activities of oil products".[64] In 2006, Sinopec, as an oil company with strong in oil refining capacity, bought more than $2 billion shares of offshore oil with 320 million dollars in Angola. Like PetroChina, Sinopec also has great interest in Sudan, "In November 2005, Sinopec Group announced plans to partner with PetroChina to purchase an oil field in Sudan, and has reportedly indicated an interest in expanding its business in Sudan."[65]

3. CNOOC

China National Offshore Oil Corporation is the third largest oil company in China. It is also the largest natural gas supplier in China.

In 2006, visiting Chinese President Hu Jintao and Kenyan President Mwai Kibaki witnessed the signing of the oil exploration agreement between Kenya and CNOOC.[66] In 2005, it topped the bid by Chevron Texaco to buy American oil company Unocal Corporation. But, finally due to the U.S. Congress opposition, it did not succeed. CNOOC has been accused of abuses of Human rights in Burma. The campaign group Arakan Oil Watch stated in a report that "left behind such a trail of abuses and environmental contamination on Ramree Island that outraged locals attacked their facilities."[67]

The SWOT Analysis

The SWOT analysis (strength, weakness, opportunity and threat) of enterprises or organizations is a very effective tool to assess strategic situation and determine the strategy choice. Advantage is a kind of resources, the organization can effectively use it to achieve the objectives of the organization; Disadvantage is the constraint or fault of the organization, and it is not conducive to achieve the organization's target; The opportunity is the favorable factors in the organizational environment; and, the threat is the adverse factors in organizational environment, which poses a destructive potential toward the organization's strategy.

1. Chinese oil companies' strengths of investment in Africa

First, it is the political advantage. China's three big oil companies are all state-owned enterprises; thus they usually have more political support and less financial pressure from the state than their competitors, western private oil companies. According to the 2010 American magazine, "Fortune", the PetroChina and Sinopec are listed as the 7th and 10th of the Fortune Global 500, respectively.[68]Firmly, both are listed as the first and second place of the China's top 500 enterprises. CNOOC is listed as the 252th in 2010, compared to the 318th in 2009. The growth is fast. With strong political support, the three oil companies have gained tremendous brand effect. In Africa, PetroChina and Sinopec are prestigious companies, because African businessmen and politicians know that the Chinese national oil companies are very stable and robust in investment and will never face financial shortage that some Western private oil companies might have. In most Chinese view, they are also considered to be the most prestigious and profitable companies, where thousands of young Chinese talents are competing fiercely for one position. In terms of market value, their ranking is evening higher. For instance, PetroChina is on the top in *Financial* Times Global 500. [69]

Besides, either in long run or in short term, energy investment continues to occupy the majority of the Chinese government's international investment. Billions of Chinese government's oversea energy investment is practically distributed and operated by the big three Chinese national oil companies.

Second, the overall management advantage of Chinese national oil companies is getting stronger. In 1998, with the restructuring of China's three big oil companies, China's oil and petrochemical industry expanded the original industrial chain to the exploration, development, refining, transportation and other business. Besides, the 1998 reform stimulated Chinese state-owned companies to actively participate in both domestic and international market as the government canceled lots of control and limitation on them and encouraged them to feed themselves. From then, the domestic sales and foreign trade of China's three big companies have been integrated into market-oriented operational system, which increases efficiency and coordination, despite this drew some criticism from thousands of fired workers. With analyzing and learning from their competitors' standards and lessons, the three Chinese national oil companies have already become modern super-enterprises. The modernity enhances their international competitiveness as well as provides vast space for their cooperation with foreign oil companies.

For instance, with more than a decade's international operation, PetroChina has already entered the virtuous cycle of the self-accumulation and rolling development stage. In recent years, Sinopec and CNOOC are speeding up the implementation of the "going out" strategy.[70] They are being involved in different scales and different models of cooperation of overseas investment and trade, by participating in project development, construction and management process. They have accumulated many precious experiences out of multinational business operations.

Third, it is the security of Chinese national energy and resource. Along with the national capital accessing to Africa, China's oil companies are trying to purchase energy assets there, and to provide financial and infrastructure projects, which attract many African leaders. In mining and oil industry, Chinese companies are taking up the upstream assets to ensure the resources and commodities, which can be seen in PetroChina's large investment in oil industry in Sudan and Angola. At the same time, some Chinese enterprises are expanding downstream activities, for instance, CNOOC is turning to retail, petrochemical, metallurgical, and power generation. Oil economic globalization and trade liberalization between China and Africa enhanced the development of Chinese national oil and resource security and the domestic stability of African countries, which can be considered as a kind of "collective security". The collective security between China and some oil-rich African countries provide certain advantages for Chinese oil companies' participation in international cooperation.

Fourth, it is the flexible business strategy and comparative advantage of economics. Chinese government and Chinese national oil companies are willing to cooperate with any African countries and companies, regardless of its international status or human right conditions, which created Chinese national oil companies' flexible business strategies in Africa. With the support from the state, Chinese national oil companies are able to do business in some very unrest African countries, such as Sudan, Angola, and Libya, while western oil companies are too much worried about the business risk and human rights issue there.

China has comparative advantage in low-cost worker and management, while western oil companies definitely do not have. Thousands of Chinese workers are continuously moved to Africa every year. A recent BBC documentary is titled "The Chinese Are Coming".[71] Although Chinese workers are not as skilled and well-educated as western workers, they are enough economic, capable and suitable to build airport, railway, apartment, hospitals and other infrastructures in Africa. The labor cost is considered to be a key advantage that Chinese oil companies have compared to their competitors.

Finally, it is the traditional friendship between China and some African countries. China and African countries are the "Third World" countries. In the late 1960s and early 1970s, China's admission into the United States was widely supported by African countries. Chinese leader Mao Zedong once said that "it was our African brothers that carried us into the United Nations."[72] At that time, in Chinese narratives, we had a very prominent commonality with African brothers, that is, we were victims of western imperialism. In Mao's China, the Tazara railway between Tanzania and Zambia was financed and executed by China and was the symbol of the Sino-African friendship at that time. Today, the friendship is strengthened by China's increasing FDI and wavier of debt in Africa.

2. Chinese national oil companies' disadvantage of investment in Africa

I think that there is no absolute disadvantage. The disadvantages for Chinese oil companies are comparative. Africa has many natural resources, but most of the African countries still lags behind and are instable. These countries lack skilled labor force. In addition, their communication and infrastructure construction is backward and most living commodities and industrial tools and equipment must be imported from abroad.

First Chinese national oil companies do not have mature business strategy. Overall, the three major oil companies lack of unified long-term development plan. There is no clear guiding ideology on how to form a cohesive force in international business. At the same time, the management of their oversea branch is not perfect. Some parent companies do not give oversea branches enough autonomy in operation, so they miss some good opportunities. By contrast, some of the parent companies take laissez-faire attitude toward their foreign subsidiaries, so it is very difficult to implement the overall strategy of the domestic parent company. In addition, most of the state-owned investment lacks of supervision mechanism, often causing unnecessary loss of companies' assets.

Second, Chinese national oil companies face great pressure from domestic energy demand and domestic criticism. China's natural resources are moderate; however its population is extremely huge. Therefore, the oil occupied by per person is lower than the world average. With the rise of economy, Chinese are scrambling for oil all over the world, which imposes great pressure on Chinese national oil companies. Besides, as Chinese national oil companies are support by Chinese government and a large amount of their capital comes from Chinese people's taxes. Thus, if they have made any mistakes or failures overseas, they are in the trouble of being fiercely criticized from Chinese public as well as the government. The rising Chinese economy also increases the cost of domestic Chinese labor. The increased cost of exploring new oil reserves may lead to the decline of benefits and motivation to produce. In addition, over the past decade most of the new found oil and gas fields are located in the remote western areas of China. Therefore, the development and exploitation is very difficult there, which needs Chinese national oil company's more investment.

Third, the structure of assets is not reasonable. Chinese national oil companies are spending a lot of money on oil refineries, oil pipelines and other infrastructures. They are still expanding domestic oil refineries. At the same time, the data suggest that PetroChina's exploration capital accounts for 61% of its expenditure, Sinopec just 40%, while western oil companies' average spending on exploring oil accounts for 70% in this region.[73] Another difficulty might be that Chinese oil companies are less advanced in the technologies of finding oils than western oil companies.

Fourth, Chinese oil companies are still weak in international competitions and unfamiliar with international practice. In recent years, despite the fact that Chinese oil companies have increased overseas investment in oil exploration and development projects, the oil filed attained by them are either small or falling output, which western big oil companies do not usually interested in. In addition, since China's oil companies have lower level of manufacturing technology, lower quality in refined petroleum products, and lower environmental standards. Their efficiency of production is thus lower, which impairs the competiveness of their products in the international market. Furthermore, compared to Western oil companies, Chinese oil companies joined the international oil market late. Thus, they do not have the advantage of first move. They are in short of talent personnel who have good knowledge of foreign languages and are familiar with international law, international business and management. They are still lack of adequate knowledge and skills to deal with oil-producing countries' political situation, their legal characteristics, the local culture and customer relationship.

The last but not least is the state-controlled bureaucracy and corruption. According to a report, Chinese national oil companies are facing the following drawbacks. First, they are driven by the promotion of officials, since the company's leaders are not elected but appointed by government. Second, their large investment projects must get the approval from government. Third, the domestic oil price is set by government and they need compensation from the government. Finally, their benefit is very large every year; however Chinese government's taxation on them is very high. Actually, a lot of their benefits have been transferred to governmental revenues. Undoubtedly, in the authoritarian regime, corruption is always a big disadvantage of Chinese national oil companies, which leads to non-transparency of decisions and individual leaders' devour of the state-owned assets.

3. The opportunities for Chinese national oil companies in Africa

Through the analysis of the external environment, some of the new opportunities for Chinese oil companies to improve their investment in Africa are revealed in this section.

Firstly, Sino-African relation is the key to increase opportunities for Chinese oil companies. China has been keeping good political relations with most of the oil producers, especially the Middle East, Africa, Central Asia, and Russia, which are known as the "core" of the world's oil supply. Peace and development are still the world theme. As the biggest developing country and permanent member of the UN Security Council, China has continuously strengthened its position and function in international affairs. Based on the Five Principles of Peaceful Coexistence, Chinese foreign policy and aid are praised in Africa.[74] The sound relationship with oil producers in Africa creates a good international environment for Chinese oil companies. China oil companies' opportunities come from: Chinese and Africans' friendly relationship, some friendly local rules and regulations, the diplomatic ties between China and Africa, Chinese companies' cost advantages, and low barriers for Chinese companies to entry the market. Among all of these, the foremost is the diplomatic relation between China and African countries.

Second, Africa is experiencing increasing political stability and economic growth in Africa. 53 African countries account for the 20% of the world land. Most African countries are the world's fastest growing economies, although some are still slow. For instance, driven by oil production, Angola has become the world third fastest growing economy. By contrast, Zimbabwe underwent a sharp drop in economy. African oil is the key for some states to create wealth. Some countries have surpassed their neighbors in wealth dramatically in recent years because of oil, such as Equatorial Guinea and Angola. War and conflict have greatly decreased in Africa. Increasing stability allows Africans to develop its economy, which definitely creates more opportunities for Chinese national oil companies.

Third, the spread of Angola model creates opportunities for Chinese national oil companies. Many infrastructures have been built or are being built by Chinese companies in Angola, such as the capital's international airport. Chinese banks' loan is also very attractive to Angola compared to Western countries. The Chinese government even waived some of its debts. Both sides know that the motivation behind all these generous actions is driven by oil, however they are still willing to cooperate, because one side needs what the other sides has. The success and benefit of Angola's cooperation with China cause other African countries' interest and willingness to adopt the Angola model, such as Congo. "China's Angola Model is being rolled out in numerous African countries. It is certainly an innovative approach for foreign actors to engage Africa—a combination of both aid and private sector commerce models."[75]

Fourthly, the development of African FDI policies makes investment in Africa more attractive. In recent years, Africa witnessed the inflows of FDI, along with strong growth, rising from $2.4 billion in 1985 to $36 billion in 2006, and remained at about 36 billion dollars in 2007.[76] In the past, the African FDI attraction is not successful. To cope with it, some African countries improve their business environment in order to increase international investors' interest. Some strategic actions are: deepening trade liberalization, implementing attractive privatization plan, making modern mining and investment laws and regulations, accepting and conforming to international agreements and practice on FDI, setting some priority projects and so on. These actions have an effect of multiplier, quickly improving some African countries' image in investors' view.

4. The threats to Chinese national oil companies

Chinese oil companies are right now facing enhanced competition from some Emerging states as well as big oil consumers in Asia. China is a fast-growing energy consumption country, so is India. India nowadays is proactively competing with China in some oil projects in Africa. Although in recent years, "India loses to China in Africa-to-Kazakhstan-to-Venezuela Oil", India poses great threat on China in future.[77] Following China, India nowadays is rush to do business in Africa, trying to establish a footstool in Africa like China has Angola there. Besides, the competition and conflict with big oil consumers, Japan and South Korea are always continuing.

Second, uncertainty and security threaten Chinese oil companies' investment in Africa. Geopolitical pressure and multinational management make relatively strong risks to China's oil companies. China's oil imports and overseas oil investment are mainly concentrated in the regions and countries where political situation is unstable, such as Sudan, Nigeria and Libya. For instance, the Sudan Darfur issue is intertwined with the political and economic interest of Chinese government and national oil companies. The Chinese government oil companies were criticized by some western media as "oil for China, Guns for Darfur". Besides, the recent Libya war also hurt China's investment and construction there. Chinese companies evacuated thousands of workers and engineers immediately before the conflict started. Thus, many projects are half-way done and suspended.

Some Chinese media reports shows that Chinese companies' assets left there in Libya were robbed by riots.

Third, poor infrastructure also endangers Chinese oil companies' investment in Africa. Now, most of African countries are weak in infrastructure. This has produced unfavorable effects on the investment of the African continent. A real African regional road system does not exist. The weak infrastructure in Africa makes the cost of transporting the goods the highest in the world. Besides, poor infrastructure can easily lead to many accidents, which endanger Chinese engineers and workers life there.

Fourth, the threat of oil hegemony comes from America. So far, the American and European oil giants are in the monopoly of almost 4/5 of high quality oil resources of the world.[78] Therefore, it is extremely hard for Chinese companies to get into their sphere of influence. Major states are still the top players of the game of world oil. The United States make full use of its military and economic advantages to build a global oil hegemony system. America monopolies vast oil resources, and controls many important strategic straits and channels, such as Hormuz, Malacca, and Panama, etc. China's shipment of oil from Africa and the Middle East must go through either Malacca or Hormuz strait, for this matter China's oil security is not optimistic.

Finally, cultural differences do cause threat to Chinese companies in Africa. George Feng and Xianzhong Mu's article meticulously exams what cultural challenges are Chinese oil companies facing in Africa and what strategies should they take. According to the authors, the cultural challenges to overseas investment management of Chinese oil companies in Africa can be summarized into five aspects, the challenge in communication, working habit, religion, orientation and coexistence.[79] For instance, the majority of Chinese are atheists, while some African countries are either Islam-oriented or Catholics-oriented. Furthermore, Chinese oil companies hire lots of Chinese workers instead of local African worker. Those Chinese workers are poor-educated farmers in China and cannot speak French or English. Language barrier actually lowers the efficiency of communication and business. Beside, hiring lots of Chinese workers instead of local people may also anger local Africans and cause hatred.

Based on the SWOT analysis above, China national oil companies should improve their overseas strategies by combing the inner side: strength of itself (S) and weakness (w), with the external environment: opportunity (O) and threat (T), respectively. A summary matrix of SWOT analysis is thus designed as follows.

SWOT Matrix Summery

	Strength	Weakness
Internal aspect	S1. relative political advantage S2. Reputation and brand S3. The integration of management and corporation restructure since 1998 S4. Relative economic advantage and enough low-cost labor S5. FDI experience in Africa S6. More flexible and brave strategies compared to Western oil companies.	W1. Less advanced management and technologies compared to Western oil companies. W2. Inappropriate structure of assets. (Too much expenditure on refinery and not enough on exploitation.) W3. state-controlled bureaucracy and corruption W4. Still weak in international competiveness. W5. Pressure from the domestic.
External aspect		
Opportunities	**S-O strategy**	**W-O strategy**
O1. China joining the WTO O2. Sound Sino-African relation O3. Rich natural resources and great potential of oil in Africa O4. The success of Angola model has spreading effect on other African countries. O5. Increasing stability and growing economy in Africa O6. More attractive FDI policies from Africa O7. The lack of American dominance in Africa	1. make use of national energy diplomacy and company's reputation to increase investment and strengthen the relationship with the oil producers 2. Increase the capital investment overseas oil and gas 3. Increase exploitation and management level, and accumulate experiences of multinational management	1. Establish strategic alliance with foreign companies to build a modern enterprise system 2. To reduce risk and enhance the competitiveness of the final product through joint venture, cooperation and development with the oil-producing countries 3. Strengthen domestic oil exploration, ensuring the domestic basic oil supply

Threats	S-T strategy	W-T strategy
T1. Increasing competition with other emerging states and big Asian oil consumers, like India, Japan and South Korea. T2. Long-term security and instability in Africa T3. Poor infrastructure in Africa T4. The threat of oil hegemony from America T5. Many cultural differences between China and Africa	1. Make use of multi-channels for more oil share and imports 2. gain benefits through competition and cooperation with foreign oil companies	1. lobby Chinese government to develop naval power, and to establish the private tanker transporting system 2. Take pragmatic strategies of international operations 3. prevent risk by increasing the commercial oil reserves

Conclusion

In recent years, China is accelerating investment in Africa, which is inseparable to the rising Chinese economy and increasing domestic demand of oil. But, the main reason I have already addressed at the beginning of this article is that to reduce the dependence on the Middle East and Latin America, because the two areas are severely dominated by America. Africa has great potential in oil. Most importantly, it provides a place where China and Western powers can compete equally. By looking at the statistical graph by Houser (2008), we also find that nowadays Chinese oil companies have greater interest in investing Africa than other regions.

Different from western oil giants, who fully consider human rights and too much worry about risks and chaos in those unrest African countries, Chinese national oil company are more brave and flexible. Chinese oil companies are willing to go to a dangerous place to exploit market. At the same time, the Chinese government is also very generous to those oil-rich African countries, helping them with infrastructure construction, bank loans, and debt relief.

Through SWOT analysis, we understand the internal side of Chinese oil companies, that is, the strength and weakness. For instance, a prominent advantage that Chinese oil companies own is supported both financially and politically by the government. Due to this back-up, Chinese oil companies are less worried in investing foreign market than Western private companies. However, this strength might also become the weakness under certain circumstance. Due to the strong connection with Chinese government, most leaders of the Chinese oil companies are appointed and promoted by government. They have strong power within the company and lack supervision and balance. Decisions are usually top-down, non-democratic and non-transparent. Therefore, corruption often happens. At the same time, we realize that the external environment, namely the opportunity and threat, is also very important for us to understand Chinese national oil companies' business in Africa. For example, the friendly relation between China and Africa, and the spread of Angola model could create more opportunities for Chinese oil companies. However, threat and challenges always accompany with opportunities. Chinese oil companies are facing numerous challenges in Africa. No matter those challenges are locally cultural differences or international competition from Western oil giants, they greatly impede Chinese oil companies' inroad in Africa. Finally, through several combinations of S, O, W and T, I put forward some suggestions for the development of Chinese national oil companies in Africa. (See the SWOT matrix table)

Overall, on the one hand, the presence of Chinese oil companies promotes local economic development and modernization in some African countries, but on the other hand, we hear much criticism about Chinese oil companies, such as the ignorance of human rights, neo-colonialism and the China threat theory. More and more competitions between the Western oil companies and Chinese oil companies are emerging nowadays. For rising China and its growing oil companies with expanding business in Africa, they should clearly recognize their strengths and weakness first, and then seize opportunities while taking great courage to confront challenges ahead.

CHAPTER 5

Global Trade and Gender Effects on the Chinese Labor Market

Since the 1980s, free trade has been greatly promoted due to the development of communication, transportation and technology. Besides, free trade is further deepened by many countries with the national policies aiming at removing barriers to free market. Some changes of the labor market have taken place in developing countries, especially in China. One significant change is that trade changes the employment and income distribution among different societal groups and genders. For this matter, the research regarding global trade and female labors in developing countries attracts more scholars' attention and goes deeper.

International trade, labor market and international factor mobility are the interesting topics that are often heavily discussed in the subject of international economics and globalization. In the contemporary world, China is undoubtedly an emerging power. To some extent, China, together with several other developing countries such as India and Brazil, can be seen as the engine of contemporary economic globalization. China's active participation and expansion in global trade are definitely inseparable to its rich labor forces. In terms of international economics theory, on the whole global trade could benefit the labors in developing countries. However, reality is far more complex than theorems. The past research of international trade and globalization pay little attention to female workers in China, and this research paper attempts to fill in the gap. The innovative feature of this research paper is to engage the themes of international economics and gender perspective. The main question of this paper is how global trade affects female labor market in China.

The influence of global trade on labor-intensive Chinese female labor

Since the 1990s, multinational companies have been flooding into China. Currently, out of the world's 500 largest multinational companies, more than 400 do business in china in various forms. These multinational companies provide lots of employment opportunities. Take Coca Cola for example, its independent suppliers have 350,000 Chinese employees. Its Independent vendors, wholesalers and retailers have 5,000 Chinese workers, and the company itself directly employs 1, 4000 Chinese. Particularly, most workers in the division of production line are female. We see that global trade does bring employment opportunities to Chinese women.

In July 1988, Hangzhou Zhongcui Food Co., Ltd. was set up. Its foreign joint venture is the Coca-Cola Company. However, two years after the establishment of Hangzhou Zhongcui Food Co., Ltd., there are more than 100 soft drinks plants were forced to stop production. At that time, Hangzhou Zhongcui Food Co., Ltd. created around 1,000 new working opportunities. However, the closure of those soft drinks plants resulted in more unemployment. There are similar examples abound in China's other industries.

Same as the Coca-Cola Company, Nike creates a lot of employment opportunities for Chinese women. In Guangdong, more and more Chinese women become Nike employees. At the same time, in Busan, South Korea, "Nike" Female employees gradually lose their jobs. Since the 1960s, the Nike Company has continued the strategy of intra-Asian migration. From South Korea and Singapore to the Philippines, Malaysia, and China, the Nike Company's manufacturing base camp continues to migrate to the place where there are cheaper female labors.

Overseas employment is also an opportunity brought to Chinese women by global trade. According to China's Ministry of Foreign Trade, by the end of November 2009, the totality of China's overseas labor is nearly 840,000, and women accounted for a large percentage. However, in the perspective of competitiveness, new jobs are always limited. To some extent, globalization does not bring more job opportunities to Chinese women, but it promotes the inter-regional mobility of jobs. New employment opportunities for women in some areas often mean that the women in other areas are facing the pressure of unemployment. What is to be sure is that globalization brings opportunities to those powerful multinational companies which are always looking for cheaper female workers. However, it is not sure that globalization really increases new jobs for women in substance.

In East Asia, limited jobs for women are in the transfer among different regions, and the transfer principle is always based on "the company's interests". Therefore, some scholars say that the current globalization, in the strict sense, should be called "corporate globalization." Globalization benefits many multinational companies producing labor-intensive products, because they obtain a more flexible and convenient adjustment for manufacturing operations. Now, they can find the lowest-cost raw materials, production base and manpower in the world. If the transportation cost of raw materials more than that of labors, they will transport labors.

More importantly, the investment principle based on the company's interests stimulates multinational companies to find lower labor costs and lower environmental standards. In reality, transnational corporations as the core of economic globalization gather most Chinese female labor in manufacturing industry. It seems that the total number of jobs for Chinese women workers has increased, but nobody can guarantee that the quality of Chinese women's employment has also been promoted.

According to China's State Economic and Trade Commission, at least in the next 50 years, manufacturing will be the main source of China's economic growth. Manufacturing industry is the cornerstone of the country's economic development and it is crucial to resolve the contradiction of Chinese employment and population. So, what is manufacturing industry in the context of China? For China, I think the manufacturing sector means "sweatshops" and "duplication of effort".

The progress of industrialization has decreased the degree of repetitive work but not changed the nature of repetitive work. The progress of industrialization has brought more human considerations to many industries, but manufacturing industry benefited little. Due to its emphasis on efficiency, manufacturing industry has the most repetitive works today. Although more and more innovative works rise in manufacturing industry, the nature of repetitiveness of manufacturing industry will still exist in future.

It is hard to imagine the feeling of women workers who tighten a screw, press a button and repeat these actions day after day. It seems that they are the same as machines. I am afraid most people will not think this work is enjoyable. In labor-intensive industries, tedious work is not the most immediate threat to workers' life. In fact, poor working environment and violation of human rights pose direct threat to labor workers. For instance, in recent years, there are repeated incidents of illegal body search that infringe on Chinese female workers' legitimate rights and interests.

We know that women are an important labor force in manufacturing industry. Especially for a number of entrepreneurs, women and even children are their ideal employees, because they can drive down labor costs and the cost of the work environment. We can assume that the employment quality of Chinese women labor will improve with a sound legal system and mature management system. On the other hand, we can also assume that when multinational companies have to comply with China's sound laws and regulations, Chinese female labor costs will greatly increase at the same time, and thus multinational companies will start to seek cheaper labor market in other areas.

The influence of global trade on knowledge-intensive Chinese female labors

We should see that globalization has promoted rapid cross-border flows of information, capital, resources and intellectual property. It also accelerated the knowledge economy pace of developing countries such as China. With the country's industrial structure adjustment, the competition of employment is no longer a physical competition. Theoretically speaking, the competition of employment is a completion of knowledge and innovation, and it is no longer a gender competition. Therefore, Chinese intellectual women have an unprecedented advantage to develop their own career. However, in reality, we should also recognize that the global trade brings to the knowledge-intensive Chinese female labor some negative impacts. Such negative effects manifested in at least two aspects:

First, the current globalization, in a sense, is dominated by Western industrial civilization. Western national standards, marketing concepts, management systems and vocational training are seen as the golden rule. In such a value evaluation system, the Western intellectual female workers, compared with China's ordinary intellectual female workers, are clearly favored by the capital market. But, those Chinese intellectual females who do global business in Western countries have competitive edge. For instance, the Chinese government issued a series of special policies for those "returnees" from developed countries. The free mobility of labors and talents in the global is an important element of globalization.

In recent years, many multinational companies strongly demand to enter China's knowledge-intensive services market. Today, a large number of female intellectuals with western background return to China. Their return releases the pressure of employment in western countries. However, the introduction of qualified personnel from developed countries is not only a "national concept", but also a "social concept". China's local intellectual female workers are at the edge of the disadvantaged sectors in global competition, combined with gender inequality in workplace. China's female workers of the knowledge-intensive industry are carrying double disadvantages in competitive global employment market, that is, one disadvantage is gender inequality, and the other is the increased returnees from western countries. It is anticipated that in the process of globalization, there will be more and more Chinese intellectual women workers will be reluctantly forced to confront the experience of unemployment.

Second, the relationship between globalization and developing countries, economic globalization is not just about economic interests and economic relations, but also involves more complex political system, ideology and cultural values and so on. When the change of values is irreversible in the trend of globalization, multinational corporations are considered "major carrier", the radical point of view even states that they are "the vanguard of economic colonialism". Nevertheless, what is indisputable is that when multinational corporations are exporting capital, they also export consumerism, materialism, and the whole aesthetic values of Western countries.

It is well known that the anti-globalization voice is also growing in the wave of globalization. From the World Trade Organization conference in Seattle to the 2002 Calgary's Group of Eight Summit and then to the United Nations World Summit on Sustainable Development held in Johannesburg and then to the West of Seven Finance Ministers Meeting held in Washington. DC, we clearly see that there are numerous masses demonstrations against the economic globalization. Although we are not anti-globalization people, we cannot put the voice of the anti-globalization as groundless and we cannot ignore that global economy imposes negative impact on women's employment. Globalization is an inevitable trend in the world; globalization can also promote the overall progress of the world. But the distribution of benefits brought by global trade to various groups must be monitored by the international community and interest groups representing various groups in the world.

World Trade Organization and Chinese Women Workers

China joined the World Trade Organization (WTO) in 2001. WTO has brought about several great impacts to women. First, China's participance in WTO further differentiates various groups of Chinese female workers. With the entry of foreign-funded enterprises, the job market of professionals and compound talents is favored. However, more Chinese female labor will be the first group of people adversely affected by globalized economy, as they are cheap labor and concentrated in the non-critical positions.

Second, women's living environment and living conditions become even more severe. The deepening of social transformation and state-owned enterprise reform exacerbate the harsh nature of the employment situation. To meet the requirement of WTO, some industries have set up or implemented new plans and standards. As the main group of women workers, front-line industrial female workers bear the brunt. Most of them worked under the planned economy before China's opening reform, and they are old and poor-educated. They are susceptible to the risk of getting laid off. If the financial crisis decreases the demand of products and thus impairs their factories, they will probably be fired and have smaller possibility of re-employment.

Besides, WTO does not change the situation that Chinese female workers are underrepresented in the labor force. Among a bunch of developing countries, China has higher percentage of women underrepresented in the labor force. To some extent, joining WTO actually weakens Chinese female workers' representation in the labor force. China is the major exporter of manufacturing products. Although we see the world today is full of "Made in China", China's exporting manufacturing products are mostly low-profitable. Most Chinese women workers work in these low-profitable industries (e.g., textiles, fiber making and garments). They are severely underpaid, and their right cannot be represented since most manufacturing enterprises are in the charge of male managers. It seems to me that Chinese female workers' economic welfare and labor right are overshadowed by the victorious surplus of China's exportation. China is a labor-abundant country. According to international trade theory, China's export of labor-intensive goods such as cloth and Daily necessities will benefit workers in labor-intensive industry. However, in reality the benefits gained from international trade are not fully shared by Chinese female workers. Owners and top managers of these Chinese manufacturing enterprisers do not give women workers enough rights to represent them and advocate for their interests.

Wage differentials

In the early 2010, China's GDP surpassed Japan and became the second largest economy. However, the ranking of China's GDP per capital is around 100 because China has the largest population. Therefore, the wage in China is quite low compared to most countries in the world; especially the wages of women workers in manufacturing industries are overall quite low. As free trade with changes in relative prices of commodities has a clear effect on income distribution, the expansion of global trade will inevitably affect the gender wage differentials in many developing countries such as China. However, at present the research literature about the impact of trade liberalization on women's wages is rare. Moreover, the analysis perspective is also largely confined to the formal manufacturing sector in developing countries, mainly targeting at the female labor force from middle-income developing countries. With regard to the impact of trade liberalization on the gender wage gap in China, there are two diametrically opposed views, that is, global trade narrows down the wage differential, and global trade expands the wage differential.

The narrowing tendency of gender wage gap stems from the comparative advantage of developing countries in global trade. In the process of globalization of trade, most developed countries have a comparative advantage in the production of technology-intensive goods, while developing countries have a comparative advantage in the production of non-skilled labor-intensive goods. The results of trade expansion make the developed countries specialize in the production and exporting of technology-intensive goods, while import unskilled labor-intensive goods. At the same time, developing countries may specialize in the production and export of non-skilled labor-intensive goods, while imports skilled labor-intensive goods. According to the neo-classical trade theory, this phenomenon will lead to rising wages of skilled workers in developed countries and the decline in wages of unskilled workers. In contrast, the wages of unskilled workers in developing countries tend to rise, while the wages of skilled workers are comparatively decreasing. As a result, for developed countries, there will be a rising wage gap between non-skilled workers and skilled workers. For developing countries, with the trade expansion there, there will be a decline in the wage gap between non-skilled workers and skilled workers.

The expansion of trade has changed the distribution of incomes of different jobs and widened the gender wage gap. As far as the relation between trade and technology is concerned, trade expansion has the compensation effect for technology, namely, the expansion of trade is more beneficial to those skilled and high-level workers. A higher proportion of men are engaged in high-level skilled work, and more women workers are engaged in temporary low-skilled work. The expansion of trade may weaken of the negotiating ability of female workers, thus expanding the gender wage gap. If the trade intense competition resulting from trade liberalization makes enterprises face strong pressure of reducing their costs, the workers under these enterprises will receive a negative effect on their wages. As a general lack of skills than their male counterparts, women are often employed as temporary workers, which cause them to have little ability to negotiate with entrepreneurs on their pay and working conditions. In economic recessions, manufacturers may probably dismiss a higher proportion of women workers, while in economic recovery they may hire much more cheap women workers. Chinese enterprises maintain competitiveness by lowering the costs so as to achieve the purpose of attracting foreign investment. This makes Chinese women workers worse off in wage negotiations, so the interests of Chinese women are more vulnerable to lose and the gender wage gap is widened. On the contrary, South Korea maintains its competitiveness by encouraging manufacturers to conduct technological upgrading and improving product quality, therefore there is a smaller loss of women workers' interests in South Korea.

To conclude, global trade is a double-edged sword for China. Global trade overall benefit China's economy as it provides more employment, capital flow, imports and exports. When we put global trade in the Chinese female workers' setting, we find that global trade has different effects on labor-intensive Chinese female labor and knowledge-intensive female labor. In general, knowledge-intensive female labor benefit more than labor-intensive Chinese female labor from global trade. Labor-intensive Chinese female labor is mostly underpaid and their rights are not fully represented. WTO brings challenges as well as opportunities to Chinese female workers. Because of WTO's requirement, many Chinese government policies and Chinese factories have to adjust their standards. Therefore, many Chinese female workers are impaired in the process. Their low skills cannot satisfy the new standards adjusted to WTO requirement. To the opposite, some Chinese female workers who received higher education and studied or lived abroad benefit a lot. The free trade gives them more opportunities to bridge China and the world. Finally, we find that there is no consensus on wage differential of Chinese female workers. Global trade may broaden the wage gap of gender as well as narrow the wage gap. If we compared Chinese female labor's wage to their past, their wages have been improved. However, if we compare them to male workers and the total gains from trade, we find that Chinese female workers share a small part of the cake in global trade. Finally, women economy is becoming a new topic after the recent financial crisis. I hope that global economy and the role of female workers should be paid more attention by more scholars in future.

Conclusion

Globalization has become an interesting topic that is often discussed in the academic sphere as well as in people's daily lives. What is the correlation between globalization and gender? How does globalization reshuffle women's role and function in society? How do modern women in return impact globalization process? These are intriguing questions worthy of discussion.

According to Laurence E. Rothenberg, Globalization is interpreted as, "the acceleration and intensification of interaction and integration among the people, companies, and governments of different nations" (Rothenberg, p.1). From Rothenberg's definition of globalization, we implicitly sense that globalization involves three diverse layers of actors. First, the individual can be viewed as the basic actor of globalization as part of groups, states and societies. Furthermore, individuals do not only experience ongoing global integration, but they also reshape it according to their interests and preferences. Second, groups or organizations are the higher-level actor of today's globalization. A group gathers and unites each person, thus solving problems beyond the individuals' capabilities. For instance, one advocate of women's rights has little leverage when tying to change the status quo of women's inequality in developing countries. However a large group of women can make change. Third, states are the dominant actor in international relations, are the third one. However, it is unwarranted to assert that states are necessarily the dominant and supreme actor in globalization.

Rothenberg also showcases three tensions brought by globalization largely based on the above three actors. Admittedly, Rothenberg's interpretation of globalization has merit. However, it only gives a general picture of globalization. Actually, globalization is far more sophisticated than what Rothenberg presents. Globalization does not only involve visible factors such as market, government, and immigration, but it also involves invisible and immaterial factors such as gender, identity, tradition and nationalism.

Our understanding of globalization can be greatly enriched through gender lens. Some scholars use terms such as "gendering globalization" and "gendered globalization". They attempt to focus specifically on women's issues with regard to globalization. Feminist movements and research is being conducted in western countries. This is in contrast to, peripheral developing countries where women rights are severely violated and there is still a lack of sufficient attention. Globalization is gendered because it provides women opportunities as well challenges. The relationship between globalization and gender is becoming increasingly clearer than it was in the past. Many issues of globalization today deal with woman equity and equality.

Throughout human history, masculine power has been dominating our society. Men's physical advantages lead to the fallacious idea that men can do better than women in all fields. Many well-educated Chief Executive Officers (CEOs) of big companies subconsciously commit such a fallacy when hiring workers. Globalization creates more employment opportunities for women, yet many positions are still assigned to men. For instance, the male politicians are more recognizable while only a few stateswomen can be recognized by the general public. Moreover, many political scientists are male. Feminists argue that the subject of international relations (IR) is manipulated and interpreted by male political leaders and scientists. So, the focus of IR is often concerns wars, power and national interest. Will the world become more peaceful, if it is largely led by women? We can make bold predictions, but we will not arrive at an exact answer. The above question put forward by feminists implies that traditional IR theorists ignore the role of gender in world politics.

According to Joan Acker, gender is a basic organizing principle in social life (Joan, p.3). Gender is gradually incorporated into globalization today. Accompanying global capitalism, women's role in some developing countries is changing. Take China for example, before, a good woman was defined by Confucius criteria embedded in Chinese people's mind over thousands of years. A woman can gain good reputation by obeying the art of women ("shou fu dao" in Chinese Pinyin). A set of feudal rules restrained Chinese women's role in society. Women's stereotypical role is generally described as an assistant to men. However, globalization is changing or even diminishing traditions in China. Due to globalization, women's role in Chinese society has been taking place great changes since the 1980s. Male chauvinism is now under fierce attack from both men and women in China. More and more Chinese women benefit from feminist movements and economic globalization. Global capitalism also shifted some large developing countries such as China and India into world factories. More and more women join manufacturing factories, thus their role in society is becoming more complex than it was in the past. They often struggle between family and work, struggle between tradition and modernity, struggle between masculinity and femininity. Even though women have more chances brought by globalization today, many of them do also face bigger challenges than ever before.

Many jobs for women are still low-paid and insecure. Gender discrimination widely exists in job markets. Women have to face fierce competition with men when trying to hunt jobs. Family violence violates women's human rights and even evolves into serious social problems. In some Muslim countries, education and liberation for women are hampered by religious belief and family ideology. For instance, the Revolutionary Association of the Women of Afghanistan (RAWA) advocates freedom, democracy and women rights in Afghanistan. However, its influence and actions are restrained by political and religious interventions in Afghanistan. Globalization brings us more wealth and immigration, at the same time it also brings about transnational crimes. For instance, more than 100,000 Ukrainian women, many of them minors, have been trapped and enslaved as prostitutes in the West[80]. Globalization received welcome as well as anti-sentiment. Some people labels globalization as Americanization. Masculine dominancy is even strengthened in some military-oriented countries like North Korea. As Joan Acker states, "in today's organizing for globalization, we can see the emergence of a hegemonic hyper-masculinity that is aggressive, ruthless, competitive, and adversarial" (Joan, p.13).

Globalization has great influence on women. In return, women impact on the ongoing globalization. Leslie Salzinger does not ask how globalization affects women, instead, she probes into the question that "how gendered understandings, assumptions and subjectivities structure global production itself" (Leslie, p.44). She also insists that the development of global production is structured by gendered meanings and selves rather than mere capitalism. Women do have increasing influence on globalization. "From stone-age economics up to capitalism no economy can function without women, women as procreators and women as workers" (Maria, p.110). Today, women are not only procreators and workers. Some of them have already become presidents, congressional leaders, Nobel and Pulitzer Prize winners, and business tycoons. The liberation of women stimulates some industries such as fashion, catering trade and entertainment. It also spurs transnational marriages. Besides, more and more preeminent female scholars enrich and promote academic research and development. Women's participation and liberation enliven theories of global development. At the same time, they bring new challenges to globalization. Employment is getting more and more competitive. Men's employment rate is decreasing. Dramatic changes of women's role may probably lead to men's psychological problems. So, put simply, globalization is a double-edged sword.

In sum, globalization and gender is intertwined. Women's role has been greatly shaped by globalization. Particularly, women in developing countries are experiencing unprecedented challenges. To some extent, western scholars' research and leadership of feminist movements have promoted women rights in developing countries. Global capitalism creates opportunities for women. More and more women become outstanding in their careers. At the same time, many women still face challenges and problems brought about by globalization. Their jobs are often low-paid. Transnational crimes and family violence jeopardize their human rights. Women's struggle is continuing. It is difficult to change people's fallacious and stereotypical views of women over night. However, there are always hopes.

NOTES

1   Thomas P. Bernstein, "Book review: The Reach of the State: Sketches of the Chinese Body Politic," *The Journal of Asian Studies*, Vol. 48, No. 2 (May, 1989), pp. 373-375.

2   Robert Putnam, Bowling Alone: The Collapse and Revival of American Community. New York: Simon & Schuster. 2000. p. 19

3   Bourdieu, P., "The forms of capital". In J. Richardson (Ed.), *Handbook of Theory and Research for the Sociology of Education*. New York, Greenwood 1986, p.248.

4   Tsai, Lily Lee. "Solidary Groups, Informal Accountability, and Local Public Goods Provision in Rural China." *American Political Science Review* 2007, 101, pp.355, 372.

5   See, Chen, Jie and Chunlong Lu, "Social Capital in Urban China: Attitudinal and Behavioral Effects on Grassroots Self-Government, *Social Science Quarterly*, Vol. 88, No. 2. (June 2007)

6   Jon B. Alterman and John W. Garver, *The Vital Triangle: China, the United States, and the Middle East*, CSIS 2008.

7   Zhao Suisheng, *China-U.S. relations transformed: perspectives and strategic interactions*. Routledge, 2007.

8   For instance, the BBC recently produces a series of documentary videos on China, called "The Chinese are coming" and many Western news reports often use "dragon' to refer to China. The recent NYTIMES has an article "How China can defeat America" with an angry dragon image. http://www.nytimes.com/2011/11/21/opinion/how-china-can-defeat-america.html?scp=4&sq=china&st=cse

9   John Mearsheimer, *The Tragedy of Great Power Politics*. W. W. Norton & Company; First edition, 2001.

10 David Lampton, *The Three Faces of China Power: Might, Money and Minds*. University of California Press; 1 edition (April 30, 2008), p.253.

11 John Mearsheimer, *The Tragedy of Great Power Politics*. W. W. Norton & Company; First edition, 2001.

12 Andrew Erickson, Lyle Goldstein, and Carnes Lord: *China Goes to Sea: Maritime Transformation in Comparative Historical Perspective*, Naval Institute Press, 2009.

13 The 2010 Chinese Defense White Paper online (In Chinese). http://wenku.baidu.com/view/915dddbdf121dd36a32d827e.html

14 Timothy Cheek, *An Introduction to Mao*, Biography & Autobiography 2010, p.369.

15 Yan Xuetong is currently the director of International Relations in Best University of China, Tsinghua University and said to be one of the think tank for president Hu. Qin Yaqing is a Party leader in the University of China Foreign Affairs and also a constructivist scholar in Chinese IR who translates Alexander Wendt's books.

16 This view comes from a conference I attended, the 2008 Sino US Relation Symposium held in Tsinghua Beijing, where I had conversation with the Chinese think tank, Yan Xue tong and the U.S. Commander of Central Command William J. Fallon.

17 Charles D Smith, *Palestine and the Arab-Israeli Conflict*, Martin 2010.

18 David Lampton, *The Three Faces of China Power: Might, Money and Minds*. University of California Press; 1st edition (April 30, 2008).

19 J Rynhold: "China's cautious new pragmatism in the Middle East", *Survival*, 1996

20 http://zhidao.baidu.com/question/57037987.html

21 Jon B. Alterman and John W. Garver, *The Vital Triangle: China, the United States, and the Middle East*, CSIS 2008.

22 Jon Alterman and John Garver, *The Vital Triangle: China, the U.S., and the Middle East*, The CSIS Press, 2008.

23 Leverett, "Managing China-US energy competition in the Middle East", *Washington Quarterly*, 2005 and WS Chen, "China's Oil Strategy: 'Going Out' to Iran", *Asian Politics & Policy*, 2010.

24 http://money.cnn.com/magazines/fortune/global500/2010/

25 Leverett, "Managing China-US energy competition in the Middle East", *Washington Quarterly*, 2005 and WS Chen, "China's Oil Strategy: 'Going Out' to Iran", *Asian Politics & Policy*, 2010.

26 A recent BBC documentary is titled "The Chinese Are Coming", expressing anxiety toward Chinese's global investment.

27 Lillian Craig Harris, *China Considers the Middle East*, Imprint London; New York: I.B. Tauris, 1993.

28 David Zweig and Bi Jianhai, "China's Global Hunt for Energy", *Foreign Affairs,* 2005.

29 Jon B. Alterman and John W. Garver, *The Vital Triangle: China, the United States, and the Middle East*. CSIS, 2008.

30 Ibid.

31 James R. Holmes and Toshi Yoshihara, *Chinese Naval Strategy in the 21st Century: The Turn to Mahan*, Routledge 2007.

32 Data based on CIA Factbook and Wikipedia.

33 T Sinha, "China-Myanmar Energy Engagements Challenges and Opportunities for India", *IPCS Issue Brief,* 2009.

34 Li Xiaojun, "On the Inflence of Sea Power upon China's oil Security*", International Forum*, 6, No. 4 2004 (In Chinese).

35 http://hamptonroads.com/2011/05/chinese-generals-tour-norfolk-naval-station

36 David B.Truman, *The Governmental Process*, Alfred A. Knopf, Inc. 1951, p.37.

37 Gary Wasserman, *The Basics of American Politics*, Longman, 1994.

38 Ronald J. Hrebenar, *Interest Group Politics in America*, M.E. Sharpe, 1997.

39 Amy Mckay, "A Simple way of Estimating Interest Group Ideology." *Public Choice*, 2008.

40 Dennis Coates & Jac Heckelman & Bonnie Wilson, "Determinants of interest group formation," *Public Choice*, vol. 133(3), 2007.

41 See, Marcus Noland, Working Paper 96-6: US-China Economic Relations, http://www.iie.com/publications/wp/wp.cfm?ResearchID=162

42 Robert G. SUTTER, *U.S. Policy Toward China: An Introduction to the Role of Interest Groups.* Maryland: Rowman and Littlefield, 1998.

43 Ronald J. Hrebenar, *Interest Group Politics in America*, M.E. Sharpe, 1997.

44 David B Truman, *The Governmental Process,* New York: Alfred A. Knopf, 1971.

45 Ronald J. Hrebenar, *Interest Group Politics in America*, M.E. Sharpe, 1997.

46 Illinois First Amendment Center, http://www.illinoisfirstamendmentcenter. com/petition.php.

47 "Lobbying Reform in the United States and the European Union: Progress on Two Continents", by Craig Holman

48 "opensecrets.org" http://www.opensecrets.org/revolving/methodology.asp.

[49]   Doak Barnett, Donald S. Rice, William M. Rudolf, George D. Schwab, and Donald S. Zagoria, "Developing a Peaceful, Stable, and Cooperative Relationship with China: A National Committee on American Foreign Policy Report ", *North Asia Projects*, 1996.

[50]   David M. Lampton, "America's China Policy in the Age of the Finance Minister: Clinton Ends Linkage," *China Quarterly*, 1994.

[51]   Thomas Friedman, "Stock Diplomacy," *New York Times*, 1994.

[52]   Doak Barnett, Donald S. Rice, William M. Rudolf, George D. Schwab, and Donald S. Zagoria, "Developing a Peaceful, Stable, and Cooperative Relationship with China: A National Committee on American Foreign Policy Report ", *North Asia Projects*, 1996.

[53]   Wangyong, "American Interest Group's Impact on U.S. China Policy", *American Studies (Chinese)*, 1998.

[54]   Ibid.

[55]   International Trade Report, November 27, 1991.

[56]   Jian Yan and Xin Qiang, "Pro-Taiwan Congress Members and US Taiwan Policy", *Pacific Journal (Chinese)*, 2005.

[57]   Li Qingsi, *American Congress and U.S. China Policy (Chinese)*, Beijing: Dangdaishijie Press, 2002.

[58]   See, Wang Feng, "An analysis of China-Angola Oil Cooperation", *Journal of China University of Petroleum,* 2011-1. (In Chinese). Although Angola replaced Saudi Arabia, becoming China's top oil-producer, China's total imports of oil from the Middle East is still larger than that from Africa. Africa is the second in China's oil import, accounting for 30% of China's overseas oil import. (See, Yao Guimei, "China's Oil Cooperation With Africa", *International Oil Economy,* 2006-11, in Chinese).

[59]   Particularly, refer to the new-built Iraq government under the supervision of American military after 2003. In some Chinese's view, South America is often viewed as the "backyard" of the U.S. lacking economic and political autonomy in real sense. These negative narratives and images about the U.S. often appear in some Chinese BBS.

[60]   Mercantilism maximizes a country or an organization's gain of resources and materials, which neglects morality, values and cooperation. To some extent, China's expansion in Africa is regarded as a neo-mercantilist. In Africa, "China is pursuing a pragmatic mercantilist policy that combines a wide array of diplomatic and economic devices." Holslag, Jonathan, "China's New Mercantilism in Central Africa", *African and Asian Studies*, Volume 5, Number 2, 2006, pp. 133-169.

61   "The History of SWOT Analysis" by T Friesner: http://www.marketingteacher. com/swot/history-of-swot.html

62   Yoshikazu Kobayshi, "Chinese NOCs's Corporate Strategies", presentation to IEEJ Study Report/Discussion Meeting, September 17, 2008.

63   "China National Petroleum Corporation—Company Profile, Information, Business Description, History, Background Information on China National Petroleum Corporation", see, http://www.petrochina.com.cn/ptr/ and ww.referenceforbusiness.com

64   Agencies (2004-02-04), "Sinopec signs evaluation deal for three oil blocks in Gabon", *China Daily*. http://www.chinadaily.com.cn/en/doc/2004-02/04/content_302948.htm.

65   Sinopec, http://en.wikipedia.org/wiki/Sinopec

66   http://www.newsgd.com/business/enterprise/200604300039.htm

67   CNOOC, http://en.wikipedia.org/wiki/China_National_Offshore_Oil_Corporation

68   http://money.cnn.com/magazines/fortune/global500/2010/

69   http://en.wikipedia.org/wiki/List_of_corporations_by_market_capitalization

70   Numerous studies are on the "going out" strategy of Chinese companies, such as, F Leverett's "Managing China-US energy competition in the Middle East" (2005) and "The New Axis of Oil" (2006), C Alden's "Harmony and Discord in China's Africa Strategy: Some Implications for Foreign Policy", *The China Quarterly*, 2009, Cambridge Univ Press, WS Chen's China's Oil Strategy: "Going Out" to Iran, *Asian Politics & Policy*, 2010, H Zhao's "China's oil venture in Africa", *East Asia*, 2007 and etc.

71   "While many in the West view Africa as a land of poverty, to the Chinese it is seen as an almost limitless business opportunity. From Angola to Tanzania, Justin meets the fearless Chinese entrepreneurs who have travelled thousands of miles to set up businesses." See, http://www.bbc.co.uk/programmes/b00ykxg9

72   Vincent Castel, Paula Ximena Mejia and Jacob Kolster, "The BRICs in North Africa: Changing the Name of the Game", *North Africa Quarterly Analytical*, first annual quarter 2011, p. 14.

73   Salimata Kone, *Research on Firm's Strategic Modes: Chinese Petroleum Corporations' Investment in Africa*, Wuhan University, 2010.

74   The five principles of peaceful coexistence are "1.Mutual respect for each other's territorial integrity and sovereignty, 2.Mutual non-aggression, 3.Mutual non-interference in each other's internal affairs, 4.Equality and mutual benefit, and 5.Peaceful co-existence." See, W Jiabao, "Carrying

forward the Five Principles of Peaceful Coexistence in the Promotion of peace and Development", *Chinese Journal of International Law*, 2004.

[75] Hannah Edinger, Johanna Jansson, etc., "China and the Democratic Republic of Congo: Partners in Development?" *The China Monitor*, Issue 34 October 2008. P.3.

[76] Niu Fang, The Strategy Research of Exploiting Africa Petroleum Market About China, China University of Petroleum, Beijing, 2008. (In Chinese)

[77] http://www.bloomberg.com/news/2010-06-30/india-losing-to-china-in-africa-to-kazakhstan-to-venezuela-oil-purchases.html

[78] Niu Fang, The Strategy Research of Exploiting Africa Petroleum Market About China, China University of Petroleum, Beijing, 2008. (In Chinese)

[79] George Feng and Xianzhong Mu: "Cultural challenges to Chinese oil companies in Africa and Their Strategies", *Energy Policy*, vol. 38, issue 11, 2010.

[80] See, *International Organization for Migration*, Piotr Bazylko "Poland, Ukraine to fight sex slave industry" Reuters, 16 July 1998.

REFERENCE

Hunter, Kennith G., Laura Ann Wilson, and Gregory G. Brunk, "Societal Complexity and Interest Group Lobbying in the American States." *Journal of Politics* 53 (2), 1991.

David B.Truman, *The Governmental Process*, Alfred A. Knopf, Inc. 1951.

Li Qingsi, *American Congress and U.S. China Policy (Chinese)*, Beijing: Dangdaishijie Press, 2002.

Gary Wasserman, *The Basics of American Politics*, Longman, 1994.

Jian Yan and Xin Qiang, "Pro-Taiwan Congress Members and US Taiwan Policy", *Pacific Journal (Chinese)*, 2005.

Ronald J. Hrebenar, *Interest Group Politics in America*, M.E. Sharpe, 1997.

Wangyong, "American Interest Group's Impact on U.S. China Policy", *American Studies (Chinese)*, 1998.

Amy Mckay, "A Simple way of Estimating Interest Group Ideology." *Public Choice*, 2008.

Dennis Coates & Jac Heckelman & Bonnie Wilson, "Determinants of interest group formation," Public Choice, vol. 133(3), 2007.

Robert G. SUTTER, *U.S. Policy Toward China: An Introduction to the Role of Interest Groups*. Maryland: Rowman and Littlefield, 1998.

Steven M. Teles, "Public Opinion and Interest Groups in the Making of US-China Policy", In Robert S. Ross, ed., *After the Cold War: Domestic Factors and U.S.-China Relations*, Armonk, New York: M. E. Sharpe, 1998.

Bibo Liang, "Political Economy of US Trade Policy towards China," *China & World Economy*, Vol. 15, No. 5, 2007.

Pan Rui, "Politicization Tendency in China-U.S. Economic and Trade Relations as Seen from the Textile Trade Disputes," *Peace and Development (Chinese)*, Vol. 6, 2009.

Kenneth Waltz, *Theory of International Politics*. New York: McGraw Hill, 1979.

James Walter Lindeen, "Interest Group Attitudes toward Reciprocal Trade Legislation", *The Public Opinion Quarterly*, Vol. 34, No. 1, 1970.

John W. Dietrich, "Interest Groups and Foreign Policy: Clinton and the China MFN Debates", *Presidential Studies Quarterly*, Vol. 29, No. 2, 1999.

Shiwei Jiang, "The Resurgence of Chinese Anti-Americanism in the 1990s: State Policy or Popular Expression?" *Contemporary International Relations*, July./Aug. 2008.

Shiwei Jiang, "An Analysis of the Environmental Policy of the European Union", *Journal of Southwest University* (Social Sciences Edition), March, 2008. (in Chinese).

Shiwei Jiang, Samuel Chester, "The Normalization Strategy of Japan in Future Politics," *The Science Education Article Collects*, December 2007 (in Chinese).

Shiwei Jiang, "The Rise of China and Its Image-Building", *View (DA SHI YE)*, 2007 (in Chinese)

Shiwei Jiang, "Where is the future? Power Transition and Social Awakening in China", *GPIS/GSIS Graduate Conference*, Norfolk VA 2013

Shiwei Jiang, Tasawar Baig, "Is Bipolarity a Sound Recipe for World Order—as compared to other historicallly know alternatives", *Institute for Cultural Diplomacy (ICD) Annual Conference*, Washington D.C. 2013.

Shiwei Jiang, "Global Trade and Its Effects on China's Female Labor Market," *International Studies Association (ISA) annual conference*, San Francisco, USA 2013

Ian Taylor: "China's Oil Diplomacy in Africa", *International Affairs*, 82: 937-959, 2006.

Ian Taylor, *China's New Role in Africa*, Lynne Rienner Publisher, 2008.

Joseph Y.S. Cheng, Huangao Shi: "China's African policy in the Post-Cold War Era", *Journal of Contemporary Asia*, Volume 39, Issue 1, 2009.

Lucy Corkina: "Uneasy allies: China's evolving relations with Angola", *Journal of Contemporary African Studies*, Volume 29, Issue 2, 2011.

Peter Marton; Tamas Matura: "The 'voracious dragon', the 'scramble' and the 'honey pot': Conceptions of conflict over Africa's natural resources", *Journal of Contemporary African Studies*, Volume 29, Issue 2, 2011,

David Goodstein: Out of Gas: The End of the Age of Oil, Norton, 2004.

Leonardo Maugeri, The Age of The Oil: The Mythology, History, and Future of the World's Most Controversial Resource, Praeger, 2006.

Chris Alden; Daniel Large; Ricardo Soares de Oliveira: China Returns to Africa: A Rising Power and a Continent Embrace, Columbia University Press, 2008.

Zhang Zhognxiang: "China's Hunt for Oil in Africa in Perspective", MPRA Paper 12829, University Library of Munich, Germany.

H Zhao's "China's oil venture in Africa", *East Asia*, 2007.

Wen Jiabao: "Carrying forward the Five Principles of Peaceful Coexistence in the Promotion of peace and Development", *Chinese Journal of International Law*, 2004.

Michael Klare; Daniel Volman: "America, China & the Scramble for Africa's Oil", *The Review of African Political Economy*, Vol.33 No.108, 2006.

Callie Amanda Wang: "Fueling the fire?: Civil war in Africa and the People's Republic of China", M.A., Georgetown University, 2010.

George Feng and Xianzhong Mu: "Cultural challenges to Chinese oil companies in Africa and Their Strategies", *Energy Policy*, vol. 38, issue 11, 2010.

Hannah Edinger, Johanna Jansson, etc.: "China and the Democratic Republic of Congo: Partners in Development?" *The China Monitor*, Issue 34, October 2008.

Holslag, Jonathan: "China's New Mercantilism in Central Africa", *African and Asian Studies*, Volume 5, Number 2, 2006

Vincent Castel, Paula Ximena Mejia and Jacob Kolster, "The BRICs in North Africa: Changing the Name of the Game", *North Africa Quarterly Analytical*, first annual quarter 2011

Cordesman and Rodhan: *The Global Oil Market: Risks And Uncertainties*, Center for Strategic & Intl Studies, 2006.

Yoshikazu Kobayshi, "Chinese NOCs's Corporate Strategies", presentation to IEEJ Study Report/Discussion Meeting, September 17, 2008.

Yetiv, Chunlong Lu: "China, Global Energy, and the Middle East", *The Middle East Journal*, Spring 2007.

Niu Fang: The Strategy Research of Exploiting Africa Petroleum Market about China, China University of Petroleum, Beijing, 2008. (In Chinese)

Salimata Kone: Research on Firm's Strategic Modes: Chinese Petroleum Corporations' Investment in Africa, Wuhan University, 2010. (In Chinese)

Yao Guimei: "China's Oil Cooperation with Africa", *International Oil Economy*, 2006-11. (In Chinese)

Wang Feng: "An analysis of China-Angola Oil Cooperation", *Journal of China University of Petroleum*, 2011-1. (In Chinese)

Saskia Sassen: *The Mobility of Labor and Capital: A study in International Investment and Labor Flow*, New York: Cambridge University Press, 1988.

Gustafsson, Bojorn and Shi Li: "Economic Transformation and the Gender Earnings Gap in Urban China", *Journal of Population Economics,* Vol. 13, No.2: 305-329.

UNDP China, China's Ascension to WTO: Challenges for Women in the Agricultural and Industrial Sectors, July 2003.

Irene van Staveren, et al: *The Feminist Economics of Trade*, New York: Routledge, 2007.

Pak Wai Liu, Xin Meng, Junsen Zhang: "Sector Gender Wage Differentials and Discrimination in the Transitional Chinese Economy," *Journal of Population Economics*, Vol. 13, No. 2: 305-329.

Maurer-Fazio, Margaret, Thomas Rawski, and Wei Zhang: "Ineqaulity in the Rewards for Holding up Half the Sky: Gender Wage Gaps in China's Urban Labour Market, 1988-1994," *China Journal* No. 41: 55-88.

Jon B. Alterman and John W. Garver, The Vital Triangle: China, the United States, and the Middle East. CSIS, 2008.

Lillian Craig Harris, China considers the Middle East, Imprint London; New York: I.B. Tauris, 1993.

John Mearsheimer, *The Tragedy of Great Power Politics*. W. W. Norton & Company; First edition, 2001.

Manochehr Dorraj, Middle East at the Crossroads: the changing political dynamics and the foreign policy challenges America and the world: conversations on the future of American foreign policy

Steven A Yetiv, Crude Awakenings: global oil security and American foreign policy

James R. Holmes and Toshi Yoshihara, *Chinese Naval Strategy in the 21st Century: The Turn to Mahan*, Routledge 2007.

Steven A Yetiv and Chunlong Lu, China, Global Energy and the Middle East, 2007 Middle East Journal

Geoffrey Kemp, The East moves West: India, China, and Asia's growing presence in the Middle East

Miria Pigato, Strengthening China's and India's trade and investment ties to the Middle East and North Africa

Anthony H. Cordesman, Energy Developments in the Middle East, Praeger, 2004

Andrew Erickson, Lyle Goldstein, and Carnes Lord, *China Goes to Sea: Maritime Transformation in Comparative Historical Perspective*, Naval Institute Press, 2009.

Kenneth M. Pollack, *A Path Out of the desert: A grand Strategy for America in the Middle East*, Random House, 2009.

Li Xiaojun, "On the Influence of Sea Power upon China's oil Security", *International Forum*, 6, No. 4 2004 (In Chinese)

David Lampton, *The Three Faces of China Power: Might, Money and Minds*. University of California Press; 1st edition (April 30, 2008)

David Zweig and Bi Jianhai, "China's Global Hunt for Energy", *Foreign Affairs,* 2005.

Henry Kissinger, *On China.* Penguin Press HC, The; 1 edition (May 17, 2011)

Mahan, *The Influence of Sea Power Upon History*, 1660-1783

J Rynhold: "China's cautious new pragmatism in the Middle East", *Survival,* 1996

T Sinha, "China-Myanmar Energy Engagements Challenges and Opportunities for India", *IPCS Issue Brief,* 2009

Leverett, "Managing China-US energy competition in the Middle East", Washington Quarterly, 2005

WS Chen, "China's Oil Strategy: 'Going Out' to Iran", Asian Politics & Policy, 2010.

HJ Mackinder, "The Geographical Pivot of History*", The Geographical Journal,* 1904.

Zhao Suisheng, *China -U.S. relations transformed: perspectives and strategic interactions.* Routledge, 2007.

Brooks, Arthur C. 2005. "Does Social Capital Make You Generous?" Social Science Quarterly 86 (1): 1-15.

Chen, Jie, and Yang Zhong. 2000. "Valuation of Individual Liberty vs. Social Order among Democratic Supporters: A Cross-Validation." Political Research Quarterly 53: 427-439.

Diamond, Larry, and Marc F. Plattner, eds. 1993. The Global Resurgence of Democracy, 2nd ed. Baltimore: Johns Hopkins University Press.

Fukuyama, Francis. 2001. "Social Capital, Civil Society and Development." Third World Quarterly 22 (1): 7-20.

Hooghe, Marc, and Dietlink Stolle (eds.). 2003. Generating Social Capital: Civil Society and Institutions in Comparative Perspective. New York: Palgrave.

Newton, Kenneth. 1997. "Social Capital and Democracy." American Behavioral Scientist 40 (5): 575-586.

O'Brien, Kevin, and Lianjiang Li. 2006. Rightful Resistance in Rural China, New York: Cambridge University Press.